THE Dragon WITHIN

Araya AnRa

THE
Dragon
WITHIN

Araya AnRa

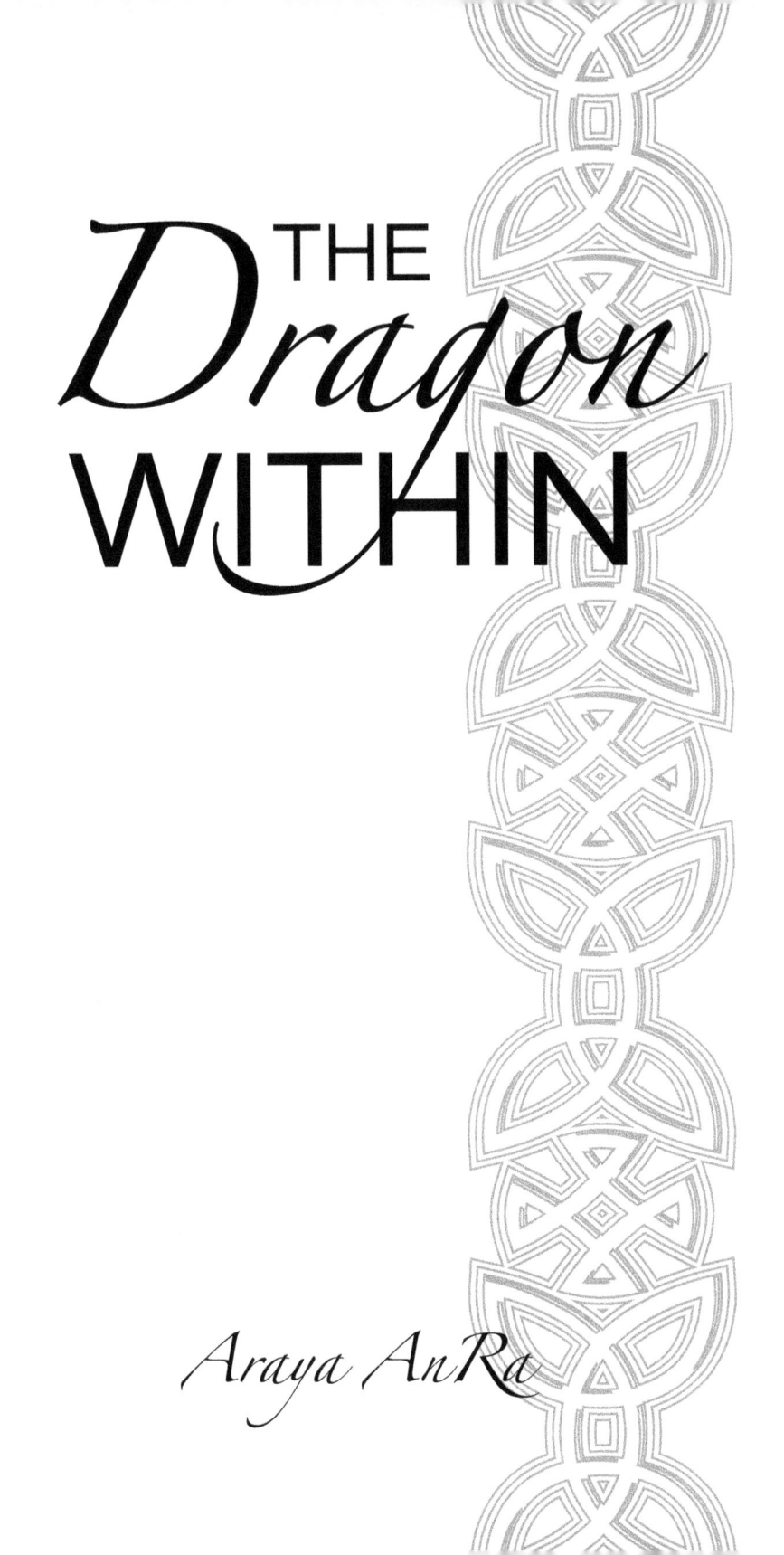

The Dragon Within
Copyright © 2019 Invoke Healing
First published in 2008 by Silver Lining Wisdom
All rights reserved

All rights reserved. No part of this publication may be reproduced, stored in a retrieval system, or transmitted, in any form or by any means, without the prior written permission of the publisher, nor be otherwise circulated in any form of binding or cover other than that in which it was published and without a similar condition being imposed on the subsequent purchaser.

Cover illustration by Mary Angela Brown
www.artisanreflections.com

ISBN 13: 978-1-7330983-0-4

OCC033000   BODY, MIND & SPIRIT / Gaia & Earth Energies
OCC011000   BODY, MIND & SPIRIT / Healing / General

Printed in the United States of America

10 9 8 7 6 5 4 3 2

Printed on acid-free paper

Email: araya@dragonwithin.com
Website: www.dragonwithin.com

Contents

FOREWORD IX
INTRODUCTION 1

The Human Aspect 7

THE CONNECTION BETWEEN THE HUMAN BODY (DNA), THE LIGHTBODY (SOUL), & GAIA (NATURE) 9

PATHWAYS IN THE BODY 12

WOMB/HARA DRAGONS 15

ISHTAR AND THE WOMB DRAGON: UNDERSTANDING THE POWER THEY HOLD 17

DRAGONKEEPERS AND DRAGONHEARTS 19

THE CHILDREN AND THE DRAGON ARMY RETURNING 21

The Dragon Aspect 25

THE GEOMETRY OF THE DRAGON ENERGIES: HOW WE RECEIVE THE ENERGY ON EARTH 27

CONTENTS

THE GEOMETRY OF THE DRAGON ENERGIES .. 30

THE DRAGONS OF MU 33

THE ELEMENTAL DRAGONS 37
- THE EARTH DRAGON............................ 40
- THE AIR DRAGON 43
- THE FIRE DRAGON 45
- THE WATER DRAGON 48

THE INTERGALACTIC DRAGONS OF LIGHT .. 53
- THE BLACK DRAGON 55
- THE WHITE DRAGON 57
- MERGING THE BLACK AND WHITE DRAGONS 59
- THE CRYSTAL DRAGON..........................61

DEEPER LEVELS OF WORK WITH THE DRAGONS 65
- WORKING WITH MULTIPLE DRAGONS AT ONCE ...65
- BALANCING WATER/FIRE, EARTH/AIR 65
- CRYSTAL AND FIRE DRAGONS 66
- SILVER AND WATER DRAGONS – A SONG OF HEALING HEART PRESENCE 68
- DANCE AND SEXUALITY – AN IMPORTANT PART OF DRAGON WORK 68

THE INTERDIMENSIONAL DRAGONS OF ORION . 73
- THE GALACTIC WOMB 73
- THE GOLD DRAGON 75
- THE SILVER DRAGON 77
- THE COPPER DRAGON 79

THE INTERDIMENSIONAL DRAGONS OF SIRIUS . 81
- THE GALACTIC MIND 81
- THE SIRIUS A DRAGON: MAY-ER-KHAN 83
- THE SIRIUS B DRAGON: AMER-KHAN 85
- THE SIRIUS C DRAGON: ASH-ER-KHAN 87

THE PRIMORDIAL DRAGONS OF THE EARTH ... 89
- TIAMAT AND THE TIAMAT TRINE 89
- TIANNU 91
- BARAHA 92
- THE RUBY, SAPPHIRE AND EMERALD DRAGONS OF MIDDLE EARTH 93
- THE EMERALD DRAGON: JEZ-EERA-BEL 95

OTHER DRAGONS IN OUR UNIVERSE 97
- THE SUN DRAGON: SORANUM 97
- THE MOON DRAGONS 97
- THE DRAGON OF SOLARIS: NINURA 98
- THE DRAGON OF ANDROMEDA: ENNGG MAAAAA ... 98
- THE PHOENIX: BEN U ASR – THE CORE OF RA, THE GREAT CENTRAL SUN 99

ENTERING THE EYE OF THE DRAGON 101
- THE EYE OF THE EARTH DRAGON 103
- THE EYE OF THE AIR DRAGON 105
- THE EYE OF THE FIRE DRAGON 108
- THE EYE OF THE WATER DRAGON 111

SUMMARY CHART OF THE DRAGONS 115

DRAGON HIERARCHY/ENERGY FLOW DIAGRAM 116

GENERAL QUESTIONS 119

ACKNOWLEDGMENTS 123

ABOUT THE AUTHOR 125

DRAGON'S BREATH CD TRACK 129

Foreword

About two years prior to the beginning of this project, I was taken in a meditation to the deep ocean floor off the coast of Peru. I was in the presence of TaNaa, the female Water Dragon, who at the time appeared to be asleep, as her eyes were closed, yet there was movement behind the giant eyelid as I stood there motionless next to her. She was communing with me without words and beginning to introduce her presence into my life. It was the beginning of our communications and now in hindsight, I realize the beginning of the Dragon Work that I would be asked to bring forth into the world.

Our communications were brief initially, mainly concerning her slow awakening and desire for me to come just sit and be with her from time to time, which I did. About a year later, I began to become aware of the presence of dragons within certain individuals when I would be doing energy sessions with them. These individuals seemed to have dragons "stuck" in their spines, trying to emerge and energetically "caught" on something. It became a part of my work to awaken and "free" these dragons, awakening simultaneously a new dragon energy within the person that they became very aware of in their daily lives.

It wasn't until August of 2007 at the first Womb of the World Gathering in Kona, Hawaii that it began to take on a much larger scope. The evening prior to the Gathering I met Padma Prakash in

FOREWORD

person for the first time. We shared a light-hearted conversation with one of the other participants and somehow my work with the dragons in my individual sessions with people came up. As is his nature, Padma simply turned and looking directly at me said "You'll have a piece to bring forward with the dragons this weekend."

I am not sure if self-conscious or unsure of myself would be the right description of my response, but I laughed it off and retorted "Well, if you get any more on that would you let me know?!" I promptly then pushed it to the back of my consciousness, eager to be a participant for once, instead of the facilitator.

By the third day, it was clear that indeed I did have a role and as it unfolded in the most gracious, organic way, I watched as I too unfolded in the most gracious, organic way. We were completing the gathering with a ceremony and ritual in the sacred waters of Pu'uhonua O Honaunau – Place of Refuge – in the birthing pool of the ancients embedded in the lava flows of the land next to the crashing waves of the sea.

After being "prepared" by two of the priestesses in the group, I sat in meditation and felt TaNaa rise from the sea floor and energetically enter the sacred pool. I opened my eyes and almost on cue, Padma looked at me and said "She's here; are you ready?" I entered the water and swam out to her, chanting the sacred language of Mu into the water as it arose within me. We then merged in a thrashing torrent of movement in the pool and then as I arose, it was she looking through my eyes and moving to meet each initiate as they entered the waters to receive her gift, the awakening of their womb dragons.

> **"SHE'S HERE; ARE YOU READY?"**

Two days later, sitting over a casual meal at our favorite table of the local café we frequented, Padma in his typical style, turned to me and stated "You realize you have a book to write now." With a new softness from within and no hesitation, my reply this time was merely "Yes, I know."

The simple Truth of it was so clear and so decisive, it was easy

FOREWORD

for me to hear and follow the next steps as they came. First, I had to find my way to England, the land of dragons where the most tangible connection still runs through the ley lines there. Letting Spirit guide the way, I found myself experiencing the dragons around Avebury and West Kennett Longbarrow for the Samhain festival with the local druids. Shortly thereafter, I landed in a lodging that was literally less than 400 yards from the Dragon Path of ancient times in Glastonbury that I had no previous knowledge of consciously. It was the only rental accommodation with such proximity, while also offering the things I needed to focus and write: solitude, a kitchenette, and a view of the Tor. When we let Spirit guide the way, it is always magical and divine.

My time there was spent in deep communion with each of the dragons, meditating, chanting and breathing with them followed by hours of trying to put the information into succinct usable form. One thing I love about the dragons is that they are very practical and efficient. There is no wasted time and no "fluff".... as you will find as you delve into the work. The explanations and background information are for the benefit of the mental part of ourselves and will hopefully be enough to give you what you need in order to delve into the more fun part of the work... being in the presence of the dragons themselves and merging with them.

This has been and continues to be the most incredible ride I could have ever imagined. I am ever grateful to Padma for his piercing clarity and for his assistance in London in anchoring in the project energetically and helping me focus it. His participation in the entire project has been invaluable. May you benefit from what has been brought forth and may the awakening of your dragons bring to light your own Path and Heart's Desires.

With the deepest Love and Respect for All Beings,

Araya AnRa

Reno, Nevada
February 2008

FOREWORD

Update October 2008: The journey of this work continues to unfold. A great deal of new information, including the presence of more dragons ready to work with humanity, was revealed during my pilgrimage to Egypt in March 2008, not long after the release of the first edition of The Dragon Within. This informaiton has been incorporated into the current edition.

As I continue to work with these magnificent Beings, more reveals, more is realized, and greater levels of clearing ensue. I look forward to the continual unveiling of this journey as we progress towards the shift in consciousness that lies before us. Already I am aware that an entire new octave of Dragons is coming into being and so the next year promises new work and openings, as well as a new book.

Introduction

We are in an era of shift. There is a massive awakening buzzing around the planet in circles of all kinds. "Lightworker" has become a fairly common term, as have DNA activations, sound healing, channeling, connection with other dimensions and interdimensional beings. There is a resurfacing of the Divine Feminine in new, powerful, balanced ways. And it is all focused on the "Ascension" process, which is really the "Descension" of our Lightbodies into the physical plane. We use sound, breath and color to heal, clear, activate… we become aware of our vast selves as co-creators of our reality with these practices. We focus on tantra and breathwork to open channels in the body to move us along our evolutionary path.

These practices are actually in most cases, ancient knowledge resurfacing in new ways, with new terminology to fit the 21st century and yet, in the days of old, the terminology was that of dragons: dragon breath, dragon mantras, dragon movement, dragon symbols. The ancient civilizations we have been a part of were much closer to the Earth and nature and thus were still aware of and able to connect to these energies. There was not a layer of fear surrounding them.

Recent history, in relative terms, has taken us away from this connection and knowledge, building a fear around "reptilian" energy and form, creating the disappearance of the physical dragons that still inhabited the planet and honoring the "Dragon Slayers" of legend by writing stories of the dragons as hideous, dangerous, blood-thirsty creatures. These fears were expanded in different cultures to a fear of all forms of nature worship of the Earth, the Goddess, the devas and nature spirits, et al. It is important to turn now and look at them again with new eyes and open hearts to understand the Truth of our source, so that we may pass into the next level.

Our flow of life, abundance, creativity and freedom is connected to working with these dragon energies in a new, conscious way. It is the completion of the spiral to come back around to the most ancient energies of creation, to our molecular roots so to speak, yet with a consciousness that allows us to move and expand into the next evolutionary phase: the next spiral.

Many modern practices have focused on taking us "out" to the cosmos into blissful places full of knowledge, healing and guidance, but the key to our shift lies in looping the Light and vibration we gain from the cosmos back into ourselves. Then, passing it consciously through the deepest layers of density within our core, and Gaia's in turn. Bringing the immense Love that this Light carries causes the transmutation of these layers before circulating it once again back through our Beings and out again to the cosmos in an endless wave – a gigantic infinity loop, or toroidal spiral, continually shifting the frequency up.

This energy created through all of humanity is increasing the level of Light and dissolution of the density on the planet that we are all feeling, whether consciously or subconsciously. All the while, though, our truest task and responsibility lies in bringing the highest level of our individual vibrations, our Lightbody, into this plane. This can only come through the same birthing canal through which we passed to arrive here. That is through the crystalline matrix within the core of Gaia and our access point to it is through the layers of density held in place by the dragons. Thus, we need to understand them, as well as how to work with and connect with them again.

The dragons have played a part in the history of the universe since the beginning. We see them sprinkled throughout ancient traditions, religions and philosophies and yet they always hold an air of purely mythic or legendary existence. Some of those traditions have held the dragons in high esteem and import. The Nagas, for example, held a place in the Hindu and Buddhist teachings. Depicted as water dragons or serpents, the Nagas were known as the Guardians or Keepers of secret knowledge. They only shared this knowledge with devotees or initiates, such as Nagarjuna, one of the most important Buddhist philosophers in history. It was during a meditation at a lake in India that he received the secret knowledge of the Naga living there who had been guarding it for him, to then share with millions of Buddhists throughout the ages.

The Tibetan Buddhist monks, as another example, had a regular practice of overtoning near waterfalls specifically to be assisted by the Water and Air Dragons to refine their sound and use of breath. Seen as the activators of the life force, the tantra Nagas of the Hindu teachings were an essential component of a student's quest to attain enlightenment. Even the Buddha was often pictured with serpents and dragons surrounding him. It is said that the empress or queen of the Nagas recognized him and appeared before him, saluting him as an avatar prior to his enlightenment.

The Christian tradition, rather than revering these beings, feared them and the unbridled, wild feminine energies they represented. With the inability to control them, they chose instead to wipe them out completely. The pagan nature worshipers, druids, priestesses, witches… anything associated with the Divine Feminine, Earth and the Dragons was burned or buried in an effort at repression. They were left to exist only in the legends and stories of myth until the time was right for the resurgence, brought forth by the dragons themselves.

This resurgence comes at a time when the return of the Divine Feminine is also ripe because they are inextricably linked one to the other. To understand this, though, one needs to return to the original formation of the planet Earth and Tiamat, the mother of form. Prior to the creation of Gaia and her consciousness, the body of the Earth had to be formed. This was the role of Tiamat, the primordial mother of form… chaos… density… through which all things come into physical form. In conjunction with the Crystalline Dragon and Metatron, the Highest Archangel, the geometry was created for the Earth's form with a Crystalline core and Heart of Fire. The ley lines, or Gaia's DNA, were then created to anchor the energies of consciousness for Gaia to come into being.

As the creator, Tiamat, also became the guardian for Gaia's ascension. When the time came, humanity would know to connect into Tiamat and she would be released, thus enabling the ascension of Earth into Light. With the activation of Gaia's Lightbody, spirit and matter would truly be connected. This cannot happen, though, until humanity has reached a certain level of Light or "ascension" (really "descension") of their Lightbodies into the physical.

As a guardian, the first layer of protection she created around Gaia was the layer just around the core of the planet. The familiar structure of creation, 12 around 1, became apparent in the 12 Dragons of Mu. They became simultaneously the first layer of creation and the first layer of protection. They were brought into being to hold the form in place and expand the possibilities of creation and form. They represented the polarities of the 3rd dimension and the elements that would make up all creations in the physical plane.

These 12 were the six male/female pairs of Black, White, Earth, Air, Fire and Water Dragons. They are the largest and oldest after Tiamat on the planet and hold the keys to both our individual awakening and anchoring of our Lightbody into the physical, and as such the keys to our part in Gaia's "ascension". They also are responsible for the cataclysmic events in nature over the eons that have been crucial opportunities of awakening for humanity.

It is through our connection to the dragon energies becoming available once again that our Lightbodies can be fully grounded into the physical. This is why the dragons are resurfacing, and play such a crucial role at this time on the planet. It is through the dragon lines of energy that all the energies between our human body (DNA), our Lightbody (soul) and Gaia (nature) can be connected. Without these dragon energies, there can be no full activations of our individual wombs (or haras for men) or Gaia's, no ascension for

Gaia and no conscious connection between this planet and the rest of the universe.

We, then, are now the ones responsible for bringing Light into the deepest darkest matter (Tiamat), just as Christ and The Buddha Padmasambhava did, so that Spirit can be realized as matter and all beings, including Gaia, can be fully plugged into their Lightbody and be identified with their soul and not just the body-mind. It is no longer about sentient individuals accomplishing these tasks, but rather us as a collective.

The exciting part lies in the fact that many souls on the planet are consciously aware and ready to step into their dharma, or role, in this grand play. Already, Tiamat knows that she has been seen for the first time in eons. We are aware of her presence wrapped tightly around the core of the planet, Gaia's womb.... hiding her, guarding her. We are also aware of the process needed to release her. Because of her chaotic, dense nature, she of course brings up our deepest excitement and our deepest fears.

One of the most fearful things for human beings is to be fully connected to the pure flow of LIFE. It can't be directed or controlled... there is no MIND in your truest nature... you can only ride it and be in JOY. This is God's desire for his co-creations, for every soul in the universe to experience pure, true BEING: Being in JOY, vibrantly ALIVE, in EVERY moment!

> **THIS IS GOD'S DESIRE ..., FOR EVERY SOUL IN THE UNIVERSE TO EXPERIENCE PURE, TRUE BEING**

And as we continue the steps forward to make this great leap in our evolution, Tiamat will know and feel our commitment and intent. Already, she is aware that the Council of the Dragons of Mu has convened for the first time in billions of years. This convening resulted in the release of the vortex of fire from Gaia's womb, which is connected both to Tiamat and to the Heart of Fire in the Crystalline Core.

This release resulted in the opening of many of the channels in the planet, from the core to the surface, that make up part of the dragon grid of ley lines. Those who are already in tune with the dragons have been aware since this event of a more physical and constant presence of specific dragons. These channels allowed many to surface completely for the first time in eons. Those that felt a connection to the dragons previously are also realizing at a deeper level that they are indeed the embodiment of these dragons. They and the dragons are one. This is a powerful realization of their true nature and multiplicity of experience.

Gaia's ascension is tied to our own and so as we work to release her so that she may "ascend", so we need to do our own work to anchor our individual Lightbodies and activate the dragon ley lines both in our individual physical forms and in the Earth itself. It is in working with the dragons and the energies they bring us that we can accomplish this.

THE Human ASPECT

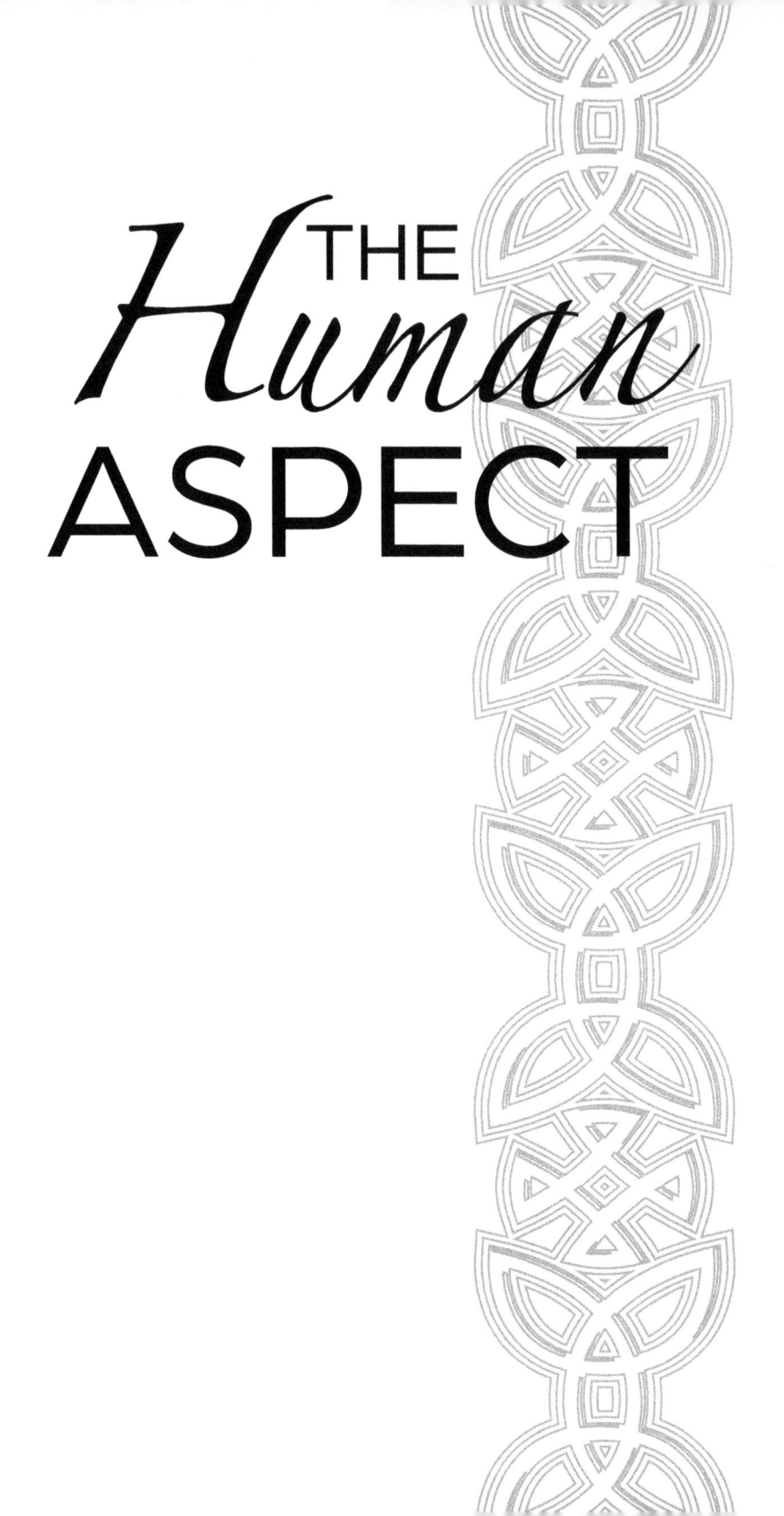

The Human Aspect

THE CONNECTION BETWEEN THE HUMAN BODY (DNA), THE LIGHTBODY (SOUL), & GAIA (NATURE)

We are aware of the DNA structure of the human body and its historically limited 2-strand connection. There are actually at least 12 strands (the Egyptians were aware of 64 while the Atlanteans were aware off 144) with the rest of the connections broken and lying dormant waiting to be reconnected. The Lightbody, as well, carries the same 12-144 strand coding, our soul blueprint, in etheric form. They, too, have been lying dormant waiting to be reconnected and anchored to the strands in the physical body.

These strands have lain disconnected while we have chosen to experience pain and separation in the realms of duality. We have kept these physical and etheric DNA strands dormant and disconnected by our desire to understand Who We Are by experiencing its opposite. In the separation from Source, there is an underlying constant seeking and yearning to reconnect with it. Once we make the conscious choice to reconnect, we create a unified chakra field within the human body by connecting it to the Lightbody and can access our full soul blueprint and reconnect directly to Oneness Consciousness.

We are never truly alone on this journey– this has been one of its greatest illusions. At times, we have felt overwhelmed or alone, as if no one else can feel the urgency or understand the strange turns our paths have taken, seemingly on intuitive whim, to lead us to the places that our souls strive to reach. As our consciousness raises and understanding seeps in, we realize that as part of the Earth, we are part of Gaia, that our evolution is tied closely with hers and with each other, and that we are responsible for Gaia's Lightbody being anchored.

> **WE ARE NEVER TRULY ALONE ON THIS JOURNEY**

In order to do so, a critical mass of Light has to be reached on the planet. As we each progress individually towards the anchoring of the Divine, our Lightbody, into this realm, we have started to find others like us and share the work we have each been doing individually, leading us to understand that it has been happening all over in little pockets, so that now the links between all the little pockets can be connected and like wildfire, the Light sweep the globe.

It is through the dragon lines of energy that all the energies between our human body (DNA), our Lightbody (soul) and Gaia (nature) can be connected. For many on their conscious path, there have been moments when the Lightbody has come in and we have been aware of its presence.

There has been a depth of connection and understanding available or superconscious moments of clarity through meditation, trance dance, ceremony, ritual or whatever practice that led us to it. These moments can be seconds, minutes or hours, but they are fleeting and the Lightbody is unable to be anchored and so disconnects again putting us back into separation. It is the soul's deepest desire to maintain this connection in every moment.

The importance of the connection between the Interdimensional

Dragons, the Intergalactic Dragons and the Elementals of the Earth plane becomes apparent when we reach the level in our journey where we become conscious of the Lightbody and are ready to anchor it fully into the physical dimensions of the Earth plane.

We have actually been working with the Gold, Silver and Copper interdimensional energies unconsciously for some time now. For those that can see auric fields, the presence of these colors and new patterns running through the aura have been apparent for several years in some individuals.

Quite often, it will begin with one of the metallic colors running in the field or one half of the field (the male or female side of the person may be working with the energy before both are) and typically you will notice in viewing the aura that this metallic field spins in the opposite direction of most of the other colors or patterns in the body.

Soon after, you may notice two of the interdimensional energies working together in the body. This is usually the Gold and Silver. One will fill half of the auric field, the other the opposite half. When viewed by one who can see the aura, the person will look almost totally bilateral in Gold and Silver at first, with the two halves spinning in opposite directions towards each other.

The sides can shift and be, for example, Gold on the right side, Silver on the Left and hours or days later the opposite. These energies will come in and out as the person is ready to receive the different levels of activation they are bringing. As we step down in consciousness or preparedness, or simply need to recalibrate to the new levels, they will exit again to give us "time" to rest and prepare for the next level of work.

By beginning to work with these energies consciously, we accelerate the process that in most cases has begun unconsciously for many already on their Journey of awakening. It is important to work with them in order though, so that the full benefit can be gained from the energies each of the Dragons brings and can activate within you.

As more and more individuals on the planet reach this capacity, so it becomes easier in a sense for those that follow. For each step we take up the ladder on our individual journey, we pull the entire level of vibration up a notch, which benefits all. In a way, this becomes part of our Service. The inner eye no longer focuses on what the small self needs, but turns outward towards serving community and the whole.

PATHWAYS IN THE BODY

There has been a great deal written over time about the energy or ley lines of the Earth. These are the ancient pathways that ancient sacred cultures that worked closely with nature were keenly aware of. Like the innate migratory paths that the birds follow to their homelands, and the whales use to guide them around the world, these energy lines guide us to areas of power and Remembering, to areas of deep connection with Gaia and subsequently to areas of power that connect to solar ley lines, that then serve to reconnect us back to the stars to bring information through for our own evolution.

Many of these lines are familiar to us because of the resurfacing of ancient pagan rituals and the uncovering of stone circles or structures around much of northern Europe, along with the research and writings many have done to help us understand them. Almost anyone venturing to those places can connect to and feel the energy flowing through these places; like putting your finger on a vein or artery and being able to feel the pulse of the planet.

Just like the human body, with its complexity of interwoven veins and arteries bringing oxygen, sustenance, and life force to every cell within its framework, the planet has its own labyrinth of energy pathways. These pathways within Gaia act much like our veins and arteries. They have the capacity to bring in fresh, higher vibrating energies and carry away older, denser energies that no longer serve the "body".

Some of these are the pathways of the dragon energies of Gaia and many have lain dormant or inactive for centuries, some for millenia. In recent decades, many people have been called to retrace these pathways and do work in specific areas to reawaken or activate these living energies that sustain Gaia and ourselves. This has all been the preparation work for Gaia's full awakening and anchoring of her Lightbody, and it is divinely appropriate that so many have taken a part in this awakening and have felt their internal call to follow their hearts to these places and complete this work.

Like all of us, Gaia's energy circuitry needs to be fully activated with the culmination being the infinity loop connecting the heart and womb, the infinity loop around the ovaries, the actual activation of the womb and its spirals and the awakening of her Womb Dragon. Her process seems to be the mirror reflection of our own, working in the reverse order of that we have to follow. Her external pathways are being activated first with the completion being in the womb, whereas our work begins from the inside out.

Similar to Gaia, we have pathways in the body for the dragon energies to follow. Many techniques in the past few decades have started clearing these pathways such as breathing techniques, mantras, past life regressions, and sound or energy healing of specific densities or blocks in the body. These techniques and many others have been helping clear and align our circuitry so that it can now be fully activated.

The Womb/Hara Dragon and its crystalline pathways in the body need to be activated first in order to re-establish our connection with Gaia and the Crystalline Core. This is our own crystalline core and the passage through which the rest of the energies can arrive as we connect womb to womb with Gaia and her crystalline core.

Once the crystalline connection through the womb is re-established, we can work from the outside in, beginning with the Elementals to open all the circuits and cells of the primary physical layers so that the physical body is prepared for the process. Working with these dragons opens the pathways again in the physical body through the torso (Earth), the spine (Air), the abdomen (Fire) and the heart (Water). Each of these needs clearing of stuck debris, pain, ancient wounding, etc. that cannot go forward into the higher vibration levels with us.

When these are opened, we are ready for the next level of working with the Black, White and Crystalline Dragons and Metatron, who is closely tied to the Crystalline dragon and is in simple terms the guardian of sacred geometry and DNA structure. This is where full connection and activation can take place within the physical body. These Beings open the higher pathways connected to our full

THE DRAGON WITHIN

DNA structure in the spine, reconnecting the etheric DNA strands with the physical DNA strands and connecting our Lightbody fully into the physical plane.

Because this work takes us into the deepest layers of density where the dragons reside within the core of the planet, this creates the energetic flow that the Mayans and some other ancient civilizations were so aware of in the journey of a soul's return to Source. Descending first into the depths and there finding the doorway to the galaxy through which souls then traveled "upward", returning along the path they originally followed to arrive on Earth.

This is the same path all of us traveled to arrive in this dimensional plane and thus the same path our Lightbody will have to follow in order to reconnect with us in the physical realm. The dragons have been the keepers of this secret knowledge and thus hold the key to our "ascension".

This activation is one of the most threatening or challenging aspects of our evolution as humans. There is a lot of fear and resistance built up around dragon or "reptilian" energies because their mysteries have remained hidden for so long. More importantly, we are uncomfortable with loss of control, getting out of the mind, being in the pure flow of life… which is what makes it so scary. Let us also be very clear that Dragons are NOT reptilian.

When your dragon is activated and your Lightbody fully grounded, you move into true co-creation and yet, you also let loose the reins of control that constrict the flow of life. You will have to simply follow the lead of your truest nature and trust the directions it takes you. You will no longer be who you THINK you are, but who you TRULY are. That is powerful!

> **YOU WILL NO LONGER BE WHO YOU THINK YOU ARE, BUT WHO YOU TRULY ARE**

WOMB/HARA DRAGONS

Each of us has a Womb Dragon. Most, currently, are laying curled up asleep at the base of the womb, awaiting their call to awaken. In women, this is within the actual womb space and in men, it is in the same "space", yet known as the hara. This dragon appears almost infantile and tiny and yet holds the immense power of creation that we hold, which increases with each activation of the womb that moves us into our true authority and position as co-creators with the Divine.

This dragon is most closely tied with the ancient powerful force of Nature, power, and sexuality: the Goddess Ishtar. Ishtar… the divine feminine, the personification of the planet Venus and all that it represents. She is the Goddess and protector of fertility and sexual love in all its tenderness and power – a true representation of a being grounded in their role as a co-creator. Her power interwoven with the dragon energy held in the womb, once activated is our connection to Gaia – womb to womb, a golden thread like an umbilical cord links up between Gaia's crystalline core and our own.

This womb dragon is also deeply connected to the Crystalline Dragon, and thus, to Metatron. An Archangel of many titles and responsibilities, like the literal translation of his name – Beyond Matrix - Metatron incorporates all things beyond this matrix and yet holds the responsibility as the keeper or guardian of this world of creation. His Light pattern translates in this realm into all of the sacred geometry we are familiar with and the more advanced geometries we are as of yet unfamiliar with.

Within this Light coding are the secrets of our DNA structure, the secrets of all things beyond this realm and the patterning we need to Re-member or Re-integrate ourselves into the Light patterns outside of the third dimension. He offers us the looking glass, like a crystalline reflection, to see through it all. It seems only natural that the Indigo and Crystal children coming in already holding these patterns for us would be under his supervision as well.

Metatron is also known as the servant or body of the Shekinah – the feminine presence of God on the planet – and assists you in owning your own power. This seems a divine balance or reflection for the aspects of Ishtar held in the womb and a perfect interweaving of the two.

Like the crystalline core of the planet, we hold a piece of the Crystalline Dragon within each of us, represented as a crystal ball encasing the sleeping womb dragon. It is through the Crystal Dragon that all dragon energies in this universe were created and through which all the ley lines, codes, and transmissions pass to reach us. Because the Crystal Dragon is directly linked to Metatron, this is directly related to our DNA structure and thus becomes a part of the reconnection and activation of the full 12-144 strands of DNA we carry. It is through this connection that new encodings will be transmitted to our Lightbodies as we evolve.

It is in the connection to the Crystalline Dragon that the internal pathways for dragon energy within the body that come from the womb space can be activated and opened. Bear in mind, this is not the same as working with or calling in the full power of the Crystal Dragon as will be discussed later. This is merely the aspect that creates and clears the pathways of energy within the body emanating from the womb so that the full activation of the Womb/Hara Dragon can take place.

For some individuals, especially those who embody DragonHeart or DragonKeeper aspects, the awakening of the crystalline aspect within the womb space can arrive almost spontaneously. The DragonHearts and DragonKeepers are the physical embodiers of the dragons on the planet. They have taken human form, yet carry the lineage of the dragons within them. They have a natural affinity for or cognizance of dragons or are keenly aware when this information surfaces that it relates directly to them in some way even if the conscious mind does not currently understand it.

The dragon energies are already flowing naturally through their pathways, although not at full force, beginning to awaken them rather than waiting to be awakened. This is the dragon breath at work from the inside out and facilitates a rapid awakening of the Womb Dragon when the individual is ready.

For most people though, the process is not spontaneous and requires focused intent. Either can be activated first. Tibetan pulsing is one of the most direct and expedient methods for clearing away the obstacles to the crystalline aspect. They can also be activated by working with the energies of the Crystal and Fire Dragons together (that is described in Working with Multiple Dragons), through a combination of the dragon work with the pulsing, or direct work with Metatron via a facilitator. Combining the dragon breath work with pulsing could be done, for example, by performing the pulsing exercise with the Crystal or Fire Dragon mantras looped in the background. As this adds such a powerful element to the pulsing, it is best to do the pulsing by itself several times first.

The Womb Dragon within the crystal ball, however, can be awakened only after a series of womb activations. These activations create a strong enough energetic field and conscious presence within the womb space to allow the awakening. Pulsing practices, tantra, a reconnection of the womb circuitry connecting the heart, womb space and the ovaries, womb mandala exercises and retrieving the name of the womb are some of the practices to facilitate this. These will typically include movement into and through some of your deepest shadows, a very necessary part of the journey. Once this level of activation is reached within the womb, a facilitator, or yourself spontaneously, can then sing the Womb Dragon awake. Singing of their individual sacred song, which connects to the soul of the womb, is the only way to awaken these dragons.

Once the Womb Dragon is awakened and that beautiful little eye opens and looks outward, then it becomes important to advance the crystalline release within the body. If this has already been completed, then once you have also completed work with the Elemental Dragons, you are ready to begin work with the Intergalactic Dragons to realize the full opening of the Crystal Dragon within you.

ISHTAR AND THE WOMB DRAGON: UNDERSTANDING THE POWER THEY HOLD

The Goddess Ishtar holds the deepest connection for us to the true awakening and power of the Womb Dragon. As mentioned, she is the embodiment of the divine feminine; the epitome of raw, wild, natural creative flow balanced in tenderness and power. It was during a powerful meditation that I experienced and understood her role.

"Ishtar stood before me and invited/called me forth into her womb...she opened her robe and pulled me in... in the darkness I merged with her power. I felt her spirals moving around me and I looked down to find in my hands a crystal ball - that which sits in the base of her womb and as I peered into it, an eye opened; the eye of the green dragon. She is connected to the green Earth dragon; Kwan Yin to the yellow Air dragon; Isis to the red Fire dragon and Lady Nada to the blue Water. The "crystal ball" is a piece of the Crystalline Dragon - it lies at the base of the womb and accesses all of the dragons because they are all embodied in and connected to the crystalline.

Thus, when first seen, it (the dragon in the womb) appears black/green - the colors all blended, but also that the true power of the womb lies in the black and green merged - the green connects us most deeply with Gaia, the Earth Mother, and the Earth Dragon and the black to Ishtar - the creative power of the Void."

This dragon energy, the primordial force, the serpent power, the raw life force, the irrational unknown, the chaos that has been slandered and denied for so long, is a key part of grounding and opening the womb completely. It will not happen otherwise. This primal chaos energy, the raw untamed feminine force, wild and free, earth resonant and active – Ishtar embodied - grounds the light into the body and earth.

The womb is the source of all creative power. When we are fully connected to it and it is fully activated with all five of the womb spirals spinning, we are in a continual process of birthing and creation; of manifesting into the physical from the Void of creation. We live totally in the moment, connected with All That Is and this is the closest state we can come to full embodiment of our truest potential and the infinite possibilities it holds; we and the Womb Dragon - the primordial power of creation – are one.

This black space is not associated with the Black Dragon, but with the Void, the emptiness from which all matter can come into being. This space lies deep within the womb and is actually connected to the Earth Dragon. It is only through a great level of work to reach the deepest levels of work with the dragons and be allowed to enter the Eye of the Earth Dragon that we reach this true level of creative power, with Ishtar by our side and all five womb spirals spinning. This is the greatest gift of Remembrance the Earth Dragon brings for us. He/She has held this magic for us for eons, waiting only for us to be ready to receive it.

DRAGONKEEPERS AND DRAGONHEARTS

The DragonHearts and the DragonKeepers are the physical embodiers of the dragons on the planet. They have taken human form, yet carry the lineage of the dragons within them, within their DNA coding. In a way we all do, as all of humanity has a dragon within the Womb/Hara space, yet some seem to hold a deeper connection or role to play with the dragon energies. This is now awakening in many as a more concrete knowing versus the historical simple fascination with, or interest in, dragon art and lore that they may have experienced.

These individuals carry the energetic presence of an actual dragon that has been sleeping up until now either in their spine, or in their heart. Those with a dragon sleeping in the spine are known as the DragonKeepers. When their dragon begins to awaken, they often go through several months of odd or unexplainable spine trauma of some type. Typically this manifests as strange pains unrelated to a specific injury or pattern of occurrence.

This is due to the awakening of the dragon, which is caused both by the increasing levels of Light on the planet, and the level of consciousness of the embodier. Those on a conscious journey are especially aware of something unexplainable becoming present. As the dragon awakens, it is slowly stretching its sleepy limbs and as this occurs in the etheric or energy body, at times a foot or wing or other extremity gets "stuck" in the human physical field and manifests itself into physical discomfort or sharp pain in the back. Usually this is in the middle-upper back (shoulder blade region) when the wings are stuck or the lower back when a foot or tail section is stuck.

THE DRAGON WITHIN

The head seems to rise naturally from the curve of the upper back and lower neck without issue.

This information has arisen in the last two years as the dragon energies increase on the planet. Many people carry a dragon in the spine. These are usually the Elementals: Earth, Air, Fire or Water, but can be any of the dragons – Gold, Silver, Copper, Black, White or Crystalline – as well. They may even be some of the other dragons that have existed throughout the history of the planet that are part of the original twelve. They are also not gender specific: men can be Keepers for female dragons and women can be Keepers for male dragons.

Once this dragon is released, the person tends to experience heightened levels of progress on their spiritual journey, deeper and more potent sexual experiences, mergings and bliss, as well as a fascination with all things relating to dragons (whether they have been aware of this connection or not), including tattoos or dragon clan markings from ancient times, and a new sense of confidence or power in decision making. They also at some point have a conscious realization that they are not only associated with this dragon, but that they ARE this dragon embodied.

Their energetic counterparts are those that carry a sleeping dragon in the heart. These are known as the DragonHearts or DragonRiders. When this dragon awakens, the first visual is of a magical eyelid opening and revealing a playful, mischievous eyeball looking from side to side with curiosity and a sort of smile in the eye. These dragons stretch and fill the heart space, bringing a softness of being that pervades the person.

These two – the DragonKeepers and DragonHearts merge powerfully when they meet. Those in relationship of this level may become aware of their dragons merging after working with the dragons individually. Like twin flame energies that we have been aware of, once they have merged, there can be no true separation even when physically distant on the planet. It is like they have always been together and indeed they have. It is in their reuniting, that deeper aspects of their individual dharma and joint dharma can be accomplished. There is a natural level of pure support and knowing in what they need to accomplish individually and jointly.

Making love with a dragon counterpart brings up spontaneous tantric experience as the womb/hara spirals activate spontaneously from the power of the merge. Even without any tantric training, these energies rise and cannot be held back any longer. This makes for powerful bonding and a perfect environment for the golden children to come through for those contracted to carry the next generation of fully enlightened beings down to the Earth plane.

Lovemaking also takes on a dimension characterized by spontaneous moments of wild, thrashing about, as if the dragons and not the humans were engaged. There can be a deep connection and knowing of this for both partners, whether or not they are both prone to experiencing things beyond the 3D physical realm. This unbridled, wild aspect is part of the gift the dragons bring to us – a return to an ancient way of being in connection with all parts of ourselves and the universe in every moment. It is the true work of Ishtar and anchors in both the dragon circuitry within the body resulting in full-body orgasmic experiences, as well as anchoring the Lightbody more fully into the physical.

THE CHILDREN AND THE DRAGON ARMY RETURNING

There is a group of children amongst us that have played a key role in reawakening the dragon energies on the planet. In 2007, at the writing of this material, most of them are between the ages of 6 and 10 and they are scattered throughout the world. Keen on all things dragon, most of them are highly tuned into the presence of dragons, can speak and write dragon languages, love to draw them and through their books, movies, video games and interests have been an important part of the reintroduction to the conscious mind of the dragons for the adults in their lives.

In talking to the parents of several of these children that live thousands of miles apart, I discovered distinct similarities in the information their children were sharing with them about their own dragons. Each child is very clear about their individual dragon – what they look like, the things they can do, even their name. As the dragon energies re-awaken and expand on the planet, they are much more in tune with what they consider "their" dragons and feel their presence more tangibly. As well, they refer to channels or pathways opening up in the planet through which the dragons can now travel freely. This, they explain, was why their dragons were now able to sit, for example, in their backyards, rather than just be present sort of energetically.

The most interesting thing, though, was the mention by all of them of an Army of Dragons that was rising to help heal the Earth. This army is comprised mainly of these awakened and attuned children, who have stayed totally conscious on their journey of who they are and why they are here. These children, by maintaining their connection, already are able to maintain the anchoring of the Lightbody within the physical plane. This is the greatest assistance and support they can bring to break up and shift the layers of density still held within this dimension so that higher vibrations can be anchored within it. It is always the children that come in to teach us and lead the way if we are willing to acknowledge them.

As well, those adults who are DragonKeepers and DragonHearts (many of them their parents) and hold the dragon energies within them as embodiers, make up part of the Army. They, besides carrying their own high levels of vibration, have played a pivotal role. For those that are parents, they have been conscious enough to allow their children to stay connected and not move into the forgetfulness that most of us have had to experience and pull ourselves out of. They have also journeyed through an actual awakening and Remembering process, which by being a living example of how to wake up from it, can empathize with and lead the way for others within their lives. The children and adult embodiers of the dragon energies together create a magnificent force to bring forth the great shift of humanity's evolution into the New Age.

©Jaemin Kim

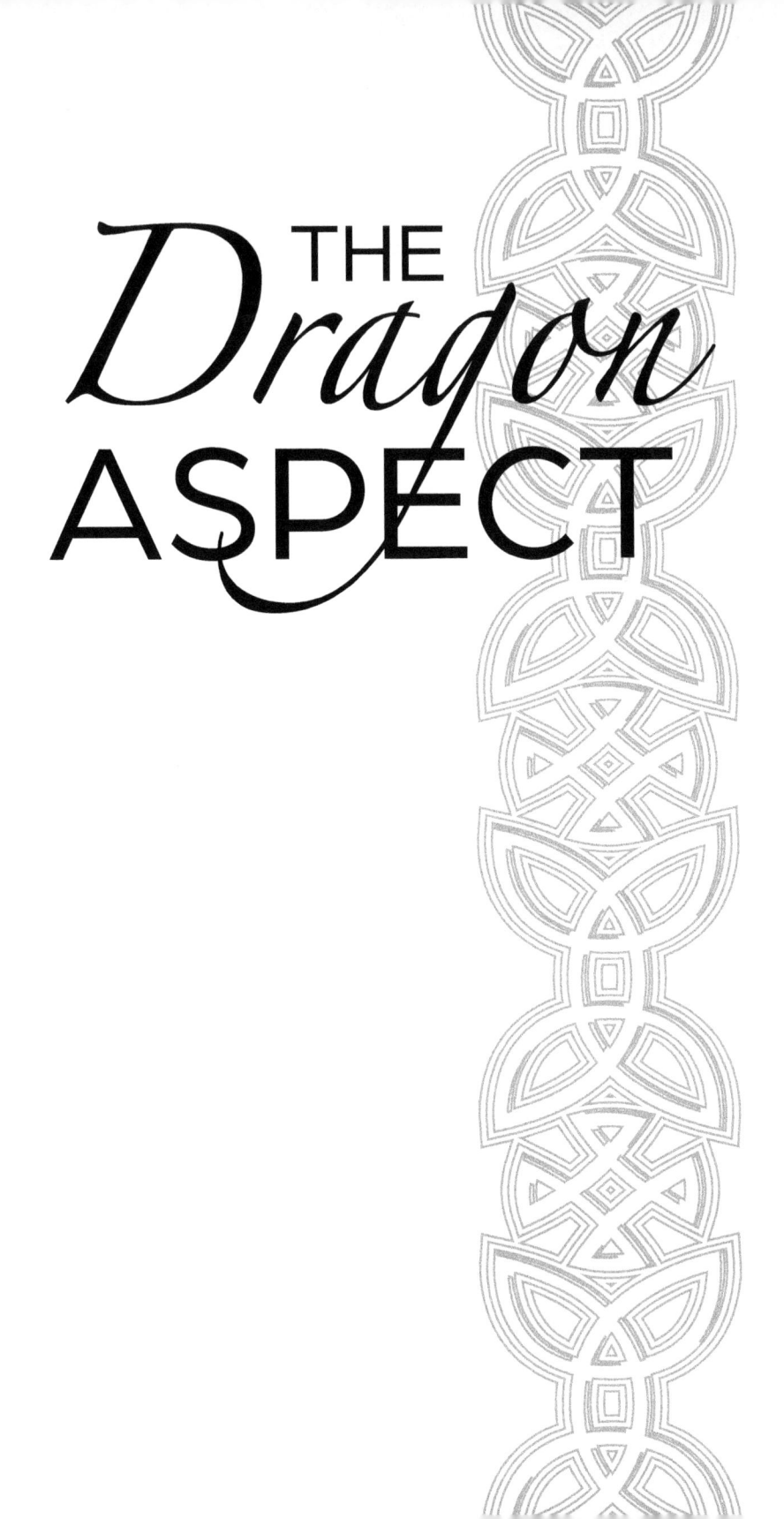

THE Dragon ASPECT

The Dragon Aspect

THE GEOMETRY OF THE DRAGON ENERGIES: HOW WE RECEIVE THE ENERGY ON EARTH

Many energies arrive to us from the Greater Central Sun by way of the star system of An, the central star in the Belt of Orion, including the dragon energies. Like all energies, they can be likened to or visualized as 'super-strings' or vibrating strings of energy that connect all parts of creation. For some, this is easier to picture in relating them to the sound waves created in music. At higher vibrational levels (or high notes), the waves are very short and fast, while those of the notes of the lower scales are longer and slower. Thus, with each step-down in notes on a scale, the wave gets longer and slower.

Similarly, in order to be perceived and used by humanity, the cosmic energies arriving to assist us, including the dragon energies, go through a series of "step-downs" as they reach the physical Earth plane and eventually the lowest density of chaos associated with Tiamat, the mother of form. They arrive to us at the highest level we are able to receive them. In turn, the return to higher vibrational

THE DRAGON WITHIN

levels (our evolution) requires a release or dissolution of the lowest chaotic levels, and "stepping-up" vibrationally.

The dragon energies coming through An are first triangulated at the highest level with the Interdimensional Copper, Silver and Gold dragons, associated respectively with the 3 stars in the Belt of Orion, El (Alnitak), An (Alnilam) and Ra (Mintaka). The next level circulates within a trine of the Intergalactic Dragons of Light created between the Archangels Metatron - associated with the Crystalline Dragon, Michael – the Black Dragon, and Melchizedek – the White Dragon.

The resulting 6-pointed Star of David configuration transmits the energies out to the four Elemental Dragons of the Earth plane: Fire, Air, Earth and Water. These are the strongest personal associations for most humans on the planet and each finds a specific affinity for one of these four in particular, even though all of the energies can be accessed and used once there is awareness of the ability to do so.

It is when we as humans join as a group with the sound, Light and power of Love of each of the Elemental Dragons we carry joined as one in a Dance of intention, that we can reach out to the trine of dragon energies holding us in the density of the 3rd dimension and allow them to be released, or dissolved. This trine is made up of the chaotic dragons known historically in Tibet and Sumeria and the mother of form, Tiamat, who holds herself wrapped around the core of the planet, hiding Gaia's womb and center of creation.

It is in her melting with the power of Love that a whole new level of Creation can begin on the planet. When Gaia's womb is no longer "hidden", her womb dragon can be awakened and her womb spirals activated allowing a return of her Divine Feminine.

In working with the Dragon energies, it is important to begin at the level of the Elementals, who embody the longest and slowest wave forms of energy that have been stepped down to frequencies that we can work with. The Elemental Dragons lay the foundation stones of our journey to reconnect to our Lightbodies consciously. The work of these great beings opens ancient pathways long forgotten within us. These pathways become the places in the physical body that once cleared will become our connection points to the Lightbody.

Once you have completed work with the Elemental Dragons, the next level is to work with the Black and White Dragons and eventually complete this trine by working with the Crystal Dragon as well. These three work with the next step up in vibration that you will then be ready to receive. Within this trine will be the first level of experience of actually connecting to the Lightbody in a tangible way.

Once these ancient connection points are re-established, work with the Gold, Silver and Copper Interdimensional Dragons, in even higher frequencies, will allow deeper levels of anchoring the Lightbody, thus allowing us to maintain the connection at all times while in the physical plane and gradually increase our vibration levels to access even higher octaves or dimensions and the Dragons and Beings associated with them. You can begin to understand why it is important to work with them in sequence.

Once connected, we have access to a great deal more information and communication beyond the physical plane and can become the co-creators with the divine that we are meant to be. At this point, deep levels of work can be done within the Eye of the Dragon, the highest level of work that can be done with the Dragons. Entering the Eye of the Dragon brings our powers of manifestation and co-creation to the conscious level in a very real way. Each of the Elemental Dragons can be accessed here. They invite us into the Eye of the Dragon to bring a gift that will help us manifest and create in a powerful, conscious way.

You will experience many unique things in working with the Dragons and many of them will let you know they are awakening by flitting open their eye towards you. To look into the Eye of the Dragon is a preparation in its own right. Do not fear it; rather honor it as the sign that you are ready to work with them.

THE GEOMETRY OF THE DRAGON ENERGIES

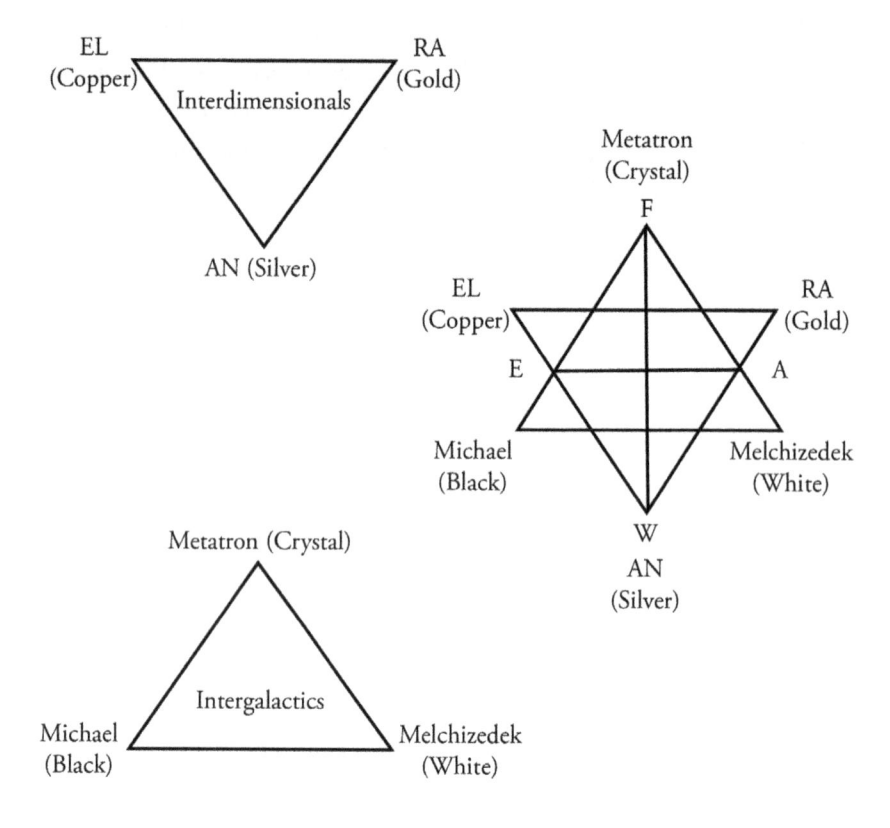

EL (Copper) — RA (Gold) — AN (Silver)
Interdimensionals

Metatron (Crystal) F
EL (Copper) E — A RA (Gold)
Michael (Black) — Melchizedek (White)
W AN (Silver)

Metatron (Crystal)
Intergalactics
Michael (Black) — Melchizedek (White)

Fire — Air
Earth — Water
Elementals

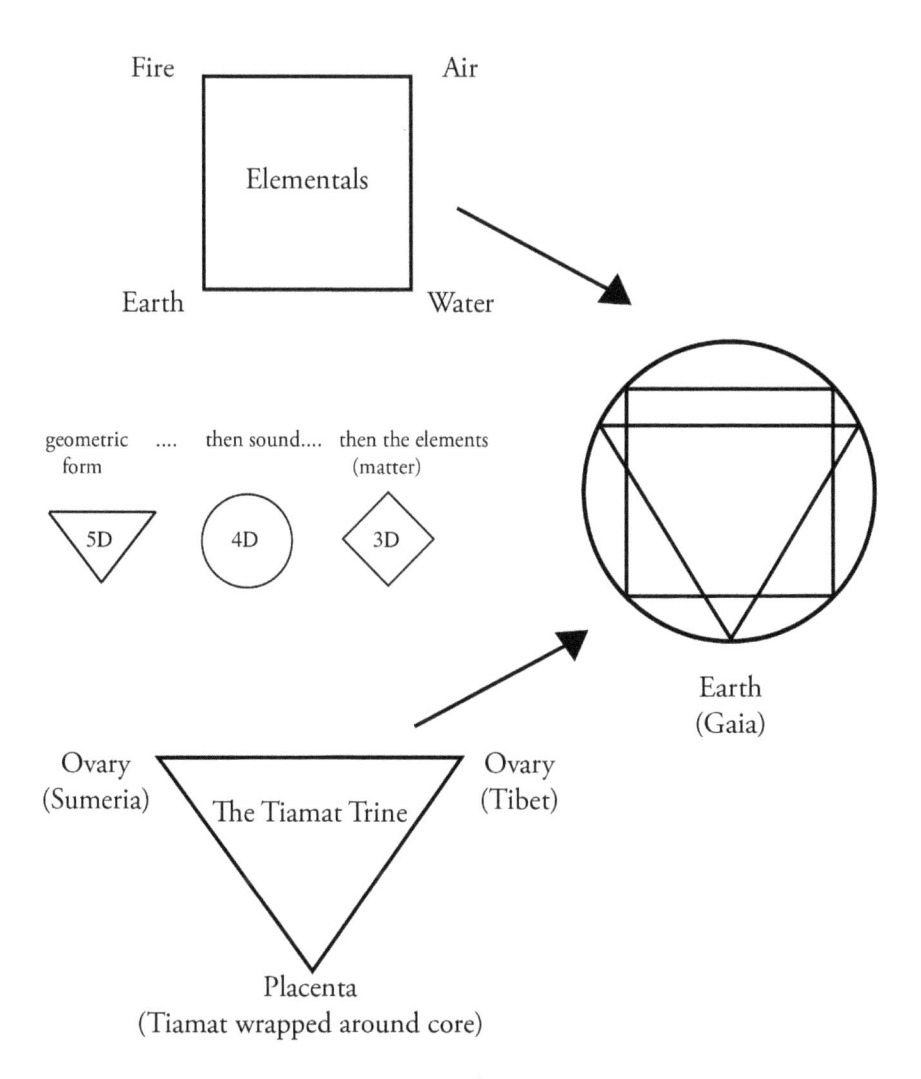

geometric form .... then sound.... then the elements (matter)

5D 4D 3D

Earth (Gaia)

Ovary (Sumeria) — Ovary (Tibet)
The Tiamat Trine
Placenta
(Tiamat wrapped around core)

The Dragons of MU

The ancient Dragons of Mu were a part of the initial creation of the planet Earth. A planet was birthed and subsequent layers upon layers of creation have been happening for billions of years: evolution by scientific terms. Cycles and cycles of civilizations have been created and destroyed, unable to reach the levels of consciousness from the heart space necessary to facilitate the anchoring of Gaia's Lightbody, which is a crucial piece in this Journey. Great, highly evolved civilizations have come and gone again, because they were missing one small key or another to move the entire planet back to the Light.

In the birthing of the planet, the universal geometry of 12 around 1 in an expansion of any form was created through the Crystal Core and expanded out to create the 12 Dragons of Mu – the physical holders of form for the Earth itself. These Dragons were emanations of highly conscious beings involved in this co-creation. They manifested first as the two pairs of male and female Black and White Dragons in a sacred trine with the Crystal Dragon. Subsequently, came the expansion to twelve and addition of the four pairs of male and female Elemental Dragons.

Before coming into form, there was an agreement amongst the Dragons of Mu to be the Keepers and Guardians of the Earth, along with Tiamat, the mother of form. First the Earth would have to be made manifest into the physical realms of the dense 3rd dimension and then her consciousness, which would come to be known as Gaia, could be called in.

Tiamat would birth her and then become her Guardian. She has been (is) the sacred placenta of Gaia's birth – the mother and the womb lining, holding in place a conscious birthing process and maintaining Gaia's connection to her umbilical cord of Light/Crystal all these billions of years. In this way, once the connection is dissolved, Gaia's birthing process will be complete. Like any child that is allowed to undergo such a conscious birthing process, she will have full remembrance and mastery of her connection to All That Is.

These 12 beings that would become the Dragons of Mu agreed to hold the first layer of form around the core of Gaia in place for the billions of years necessary until the civilizations of the planet (humanity) would be ready to help Gaia herself anchor her Lightbody. The Council of Twelve was very specific that they would not reconvene until the time was truly ripe.

Indeed, they were to help destroy and dissolve civilizations if things were evolving in the wrong way. Many of the disastrous Earth phenomena that felled entire civilizations, like those in Lemuria or Atlantis were brought about by the tremulous movements of these twelve giants. They reside within the tectonic plates of the earth's crust, with their spines and/or tails in most cases running along the border zones between plates.[1]

These plates over eons having been pushing against or pulling away from each other creating the mountains and deep ocean rifts that are part of our global geography. Most shifts have been a natural gradual evolution, taking eons, with each slight movement being felt as an earthquake or tremor on land or creating waves from the ocean floor that at times have become tsunamis or tidal waves by

---

[1] The 1994 National Geographic Society Physical Map of the World is the best map to view this phenomenon as it details both the mountainous ridge formations above and below sea level and the layout of the tectonic plates.

landfall. Others have been initiated by the dragons and have been much more devastating.

In the last council held before coming into form, the Female Water Dragon was elected by the Council to be responsible for incarnating in human form and bringing forth not only the information from the Dragons, but to reconvene the Council. This meant that as the end of an age was reached, she would have to be incarnate in human form in order to convene the Council if necessary based on humanity's progress. If humanity were ready, she would reconvene the Council by her call.

This call would be echoed through the core of the Earth so that all the Dragons would feel it and know to arrive. She would know it was time by a sign from humanity that a certain level of Light and commitment had been reached in the mass consciousness and all things would align effortlessly to put her in the right spot at the right time to send out the code.

With the reconvening of the Council for the first time in billions of years, it would still take a unanimous decision to move forward with the bringing forth of the ancient information and to what degree humanity would need some "assistance" or "shake up" to really unite fully. The agreement was reached in the reconvening of the Council in September of 2007 that indeed humanity had surpassed the levels of Light expected at this point and would need very little physical "shake up" to progress.

Many humans, deeply connected to these lineages, feel the stirrings of something ancient, deep and possibly unexplainable within them. Others are incarnate aspects of the dragon lineages themselves and are starting to feel a pull to these beings, unsure why this new fascination is arising, but clear of its power. Most of this is being brought on through the Dragon Children and the games and fascinations they bring into the households of their, most likely, dragon lineage parents.

Some are experiencing connections to the many hundreds of types of dragons that have been birthed since the creation of the Dragons of Mu. These are all lineages from them - their ancestral tree - and there have been many. From the small newts and salamanders of the breed to the larger Komodo dragons to the dragons that roamed the planet for centuries before being hunted and slain in fear. So misunderstood were they that they vanished into the mists if they were not slain. So you may be connected to a dragon not mentioned in this text – pink dragons, rainbow dragons, black and gold blended dragons, purple dragons, turquoise dragons… you may also experience some of the dragons around the globe that are guardians of specific regions and are awakening. They all can be traced back through their lineages to the original twelve which are the ones we need to access for the work to be done. Whatever the means that one discovers the connection, it is ancient and real work that will facilitate your Journey Home.

The Elemental Dragons

There are four Elemental Dragons of the Earth plane: Earth, Air, Fire and Water. These are the strongest personal associations for most of us on the planet, and each one of us finds a specific affinity for one of these four in particular, even though all of the energies can be accessed and used once there is awareness of the ability to do so. The deep kinship or association one feels with one of the elemental dragons does not necessarily relate to one's birth sign. For example, a Libra is considered an Air sign, but may be most influenced by the Water Dragon.

These dragons are our connection to the dragon lines of energy within the physical body and as such, our connection to expanding ourselves into freedom and full consciousness in the physical. By connecting to and merging with them, the Black and White Dragons can be connected to, which in turn leads to our expansion through the Crystal Dragon and into the interdimensional dragon lines of transmission through the core of the planet and Metatron.

There is natural balance within the dragon geometry as we merge and use them. Not only is there balance to be found in the merging of the male and female aspects of one particular type of dragon, but other pairings can be merged as well. For example, the Earth and Air dragons merge and support each other as do the Fire and

Water dragons. To work with multiple dragons, it is most useful to work with either already merged energies (male/female) of each type (Earth, Air, Fire or Water) or work with, for example, the male Earth and the female Air or the female Water and male Fire. There are different aspects to be anchored and experienced with the male and female energies of each and working with them together, as described in the section Working With Multiple Dragons at Once.) Begin your work with the dragons, however, individually, focusing on either the male or female aspect of each.

It is through sound, breath, movement, and the harnessing of sexual energy that we connect to, and feel them awaken within us. We feel the transformation as the Dragon Within awakens and breathes through us. The breath changes becoming more raspy, deeper, fuller, hotter… the eyes flutter open intermittently and we look upon the world in a new way as if seeing it for the first time; feeling the Dragon looking through our eyes. The body begins to sway and move spontaneously, stretching in new ways as if stretching sleeping muscles and joints that have been still for eons.

Working with the Dragons allows new circuits to begin to flow that create heat throughout the body letting us know of their presence. When these four are awakened within and merged, the White and Black Dragons can be accessed to reach an even deeper level.

Begin with the dragon that speaks to you most loudly as you hold all four in front of you. Spend time with only one, really anchoring it deeply within you and merging with it before working with the next. Listen first to the individual CD track for that dragon's mantra to ensure the right rhythm and pronunciation and then spend time sounding it alone. Once you have worked with the dragons' sounds for yourself, you can move into deeper levels of work with them by looping the CD tracks, so that they continue in the background as you move into a deeper internal space in the presence of the dragon you are working with.

When sounding the mantras for yourself, it is important to sound it verbally and not just internally to feel the expulsion of the breath and the dragon rising within. Allow the movements to flow freely from this space through the body. The Earth Dragon, for example, may move differently through each person's body, although the breath expulsion patterns described for each will be consistent. Allow this part to be organic and creative… that is one of the keys of the dragons. If you feel moved to dance with them, dance.

Once a deep space of connection has been reached, then tune in and feel whether you have connected to the male or female aspect of this particular Elemental Dragon. The first one you connect to is a deep connection for you and one that will be like your foundation stone. Women can be Keepers of male dragon energies, as can men be Keepers of female dragon energies.

For each of the elements there will be different experiences with the male and female aspects, and different circuitry in the body activated. When both have been worked with individually, you can set your intention and ask to have them merge within you. This merging is a very powerful experience with any of the Dragons. It is like experiencing them making ecstatic love in, around and through you. They revel in it, as will you.

It will be helpful as you work with these energies to also envision or have an image of the symbol for each dragon with you, as well as, if possible, a piece of the stone or metal they are associated with. This will make the connection stronger and easier to access, especially when working alone. Group or partner breathing and sounding, like meditation, offers an exponential energetic component to enhance the energy flow coming through.

You may also experience spontaneous work with the dragons once a connection has been made during your sleep. They like to work in the realms we access during deep REM sleep because we are more open and receptive in those realms. Do not worry if you cannot bring the experience back with you; just try to remember which dragons you were working with and maybe keep a journal of it for later reference.

Your work with the Elemental Dragons is the first layer of connection and awakening of ancient pathways through the body and the foundation for the eventual anchoring of the Lightbody into the physical that the Interdimensional Dragons bring to you. Take your time with it as you would the laying of any foundation. This will make the subsequent work not only deeper, but actually possible, as the Dragons will not work with you at certain levels if you are not properly prepared.

This especially applies to the true gifts the Elemental Dragons bring when you reach the level of working in the Eye of the Dragon. Work in this realm allows us to reach our co-creative divinity and regain access to streams of divine consciousness and the keys to manifesting consciously in order to bring Spirit into Matter. It is well worth laying a solid foundation in order to reach this level of work.

THE EARTH DRAGON

- » Associated with Ishtar
- » Function: the activator of wild, orgasmic, powerful energy flows in the body and the grounder of manifestation into the physical
- » Stone: Moldovite
- » Metal: Copper
- » Mantra: Mee Tu Am Na Hey Rua

The Earth Dragon holds the most power for us to ground the Lightbody fully into the physical, as well as to ground our intentions and creations into the physical. He/She is a magnificent serpent-like creature of deep brownish-green living below the earth's surface. The male Earth Dragon of Mu resides in South America stretched from Argentina to the Caribbean Islands, while his female counterpart covers most of eastern Australia with her tail extending up into the deep ocean trench east of the Asian continent.

To work with the Earth Dragons, sit in a comfortable position. Envision being led to a small cave deep in the earth. There is a dim light available although it is not made by any source you are aware of. Sit in the cave and begin to breathe. When the breath begins to feel raspy and low, like that of a dragon, begin to chant the mantra deeply on an exhalation. The full mantra will be chanted with each inhalation and exhalation as a continuous sounding.

Ask your inner guide whether you would like to call forth the male or female Earth Dragon first or simply allow the one who desires to work with you to step forward. If you have worked with both individually, you can call forth the experience to have them merge within you.

You will find when working with the male Earth Dragon, that your breath wants to be pushed across the floor of the cave and your body may begin to sway in side-to-side figure eights in a serpentine motion. As the energy increases and the mantra gets sounded more powerfully, you will feel energy descend across the shoulders and down the back to the hamstrings, as if He is standing behind you breathing down your back. These are the channels he opens up for you. They carry physical strength and grounding, as well as the grounding of new creations and manifestations you are trying to bring into your physical reality.

The female Earth Dragon, when you are ready to work with her, will guide the breath in a circular pattern exhaling and sending it across the roof of the cave. Moving the head in a counter-clockwise circle, breathing the mantra in on the downswing and exhaling while sounding the mantra out as the head arcs slowly across the upper half of the circle. This creates a vortex of energy to bring creations through to be held like an egg at the base of the abdomen, directly in front of the womb or hara space. (See the advanced work described in Entering the Eye of the Earth Dragon) You will feel the energy circuits on the front of the body open up from the pectoral muscles across the front of the chest down to about mid-thigh.

The male especially empowers one with a sense of knowing and surety in physical realm decisions, while the female offers a boost in confidence and self-esteem (the surety of decisions for the self vs. the world). They both are helping anchor the central portion of the Lightbody to the core of the physical body across the entire torso. This will manifest in feeling lighter, yet more solid, and grounded.

Continue to breathe, chanting the mantra, trying to synchronize your inhalations and exhalations with the Earth Dragon's breath.

Continue chanting and breathing for at least 10 minutes focusing on the feelings and sensations pulsing up and down the front or back of the torso, depending on which aspect you are working with. At some point, as you move into a very deep space, you can allow the mantra to become an internal, non-verbal process. The breath will remain heavy, deep and in synch with that of the Earth Dragon.

The longer you can stay with this exercise, the more alive and expanded these pathways will become. You will feel them tingling and coming to life. Work with each of the male and female Earth Dragons in this way to expand and open these ancient pathways before merging them. The more you work with them, the more anchored this energy will become within you and the easier to keep these channels open and flowing. This will begin to manifest in the surety in decision-making and self-esteem they carry on a regular basis in your life.

Until then, you can also use them in very real ways to boost those aspects until they are fully anchored. It will be useful to work, for example, with the male Earth Dragon before you sit with a decision that needs to be made in your life. Similarly, open the channels of the female Earth Dragon before you do things that make you nervous like public speaking, job interviews or visiting the in-laws.

After you have worked with both the male and female aspects of the Earth Dragon individually, you will want to merge them within you. For this to occur, begin in the same way and then individually bring them in one at a time until you feel the familiar pathways they open become alive and activated on both the front and back of the torso. Then ask them to merge within you and continue breathing and chanting internally with them until you feel them move towards each other.

The merging will open further pathways within the torso connecting key points of the front and back of the body, especially through the womb/hara space. It will feel like an internal explosion or full body orgasm as these connections re-fire for the first time. Once again, stay with the breath as long as you can to deepen and open these connections further. Revel in the ecstasy of the experience knowing that this bliss is the inheritance of your divine birthright and all the beings in the universe revel with you as the anchor points of your Lightbody take hold!

As you complete any session with the Earth Dragons, let the mantra cease, let your breathing come back to normal and sit in the cave integrating it all. Then thank them for the work they have done with you before returning to the physical space around you.

THE AIR DRAGON

» Associated with Kwan Yin
» Function: main carrier into consciousness through compassion
» Stone: Amber and Yellow Topaz
» Metal: Brass
» Mantra: Mee Ru Ah Tu Nay Ah Oh

The Air Dragon creates massive vortexes between the heavens and earth to transfer information and energy between the two into consciousness. These create upheaval and clearing on a massive scale both personally and planetarily. The Air Dragons create the hurricanes and typhoons on the planet to bring consciousness and shift to areas of dense energy… breaking up, transforming, and imbuing with new levels of consciousness and community.

The Air Dragons are powerful beings with massive wings and large bodies of a yellowish-orange luster. The male Air Dragon of Mu extends through most of the China coastline and up into the northernmost regions of Siberia. The female holds in position the eastern regions of North America from the Appalachian range all the way to the Elizabeth Islands of Canada.

To work with the Air Dragons visualize sitting on a cloud halfway between the heavens and the Earth. Begin chanting the mantra and feel your head lift either skyward or towards the Earth. If your head goes skyward, you are working with the female Air Dragon. Your head will naturally flow in an anti-clockwise circle as if drawing a large circle with the breath all the way around the heavens.

As the mantra continues, a great vortex will open up and you will feel it gradually increase in speed and size, funneling into the crown chakra. This is the direct path for new consciousness to arrive into your Lightbody when it is fully anchored. You will begin work with this when you move into working in the Eye of the Air Dragon.

Working with the male Air Dragon, you will find your breath drawing a similar anti-clockwise circle downward encompassing the earth and creating a similar, although perfectly mirrored vortex from the Earth up into the root chakra. This will bring a surge of communication through the lower chakras and the core of the planet.

Continue chanting the mantra and breathing into the vortex, empowering it to spin higher, wider and faster until you feel or sense a pillar of energy entering the core of the vortex either from the heavens or from the core of the planet. As it does so, you will feel a natural point to let go of the mantra and just move into a deep meditative space within the vortex.

Whether it is with the female Air Dragon in the crown or the male in the root, feel the pillar of energy move downward or upward through the vortex and into the spine as deeply as it will go. It should stop just above or below the heart chakra. Repeat your work with the Air Dragons individually until it does so before attempting to merge them. Stay in this space feeling the pulsing of the pillar of energy now within your spine expanding and opening the circuitry of this ancient pathway. When you feel the energy begin to dissipate bring your awareness back to the physical body and the room around you.

When you are ready to merge the Air Dragons, begin in the same way, bringing in either the male or female aspect. Once the vortex is spinning rapidly, repeat the mantra and breath pattern to bring in the opposite aspect. The two together create an hourglass type configuration with you in the center, both halves spinning anti-clockwise into the center where they meet.

Bring your breath into the center, continuing to chant the mantra and visualizing the vortexes spinning higher, wider and faster simultaneously. You will experience the familiar pillars of energy enter the vortexes from either side and begin towards each other within the spine. Continue the mantra as long as you can as they move towards each other.

When the two merge, there will be a tingling and opening along the entire spine, similar to an experience of kundalini rising, yet much more powerful. This exercise can tend to make you feel light-headed or dizzy, so it is best to do in a seated posture and to have a small plate of food nearby, already prepared, to ground you after the experience; chocolate and bread are excellent for this. The more you practice it and open this channel, the less physical side effects you will experience.

Stay with this experience as long as you can before returning your focus to the body and the room around you. Sit quietly as you integrate the new levels of energy pulsing through the spine and chakra channels. Do not try to get up too quickly or rush off to do things in the world. Plan this session with ample time to just be within this energy. It will be something to adjust to.

THE FIRE DRAGON

» Associated with Isis
» Function: main power source to fuel expression and manifestation
» Stone: Carnelian
» Metal: Iron
» Mantra: Bah Tu Haa Beesh Tau Hay

The Fire Dragon ignites the core and burns up our fears, blockages, and ancient karmic blocks stuck in the lower chakras. This includes the burning up and clearing of all birth traumas and chemicals still stuck in the body from being birthed with the unconscious practices of the past millenia. We all have very real biochemical substances accumulated in the body over lifetimes from suffering, fear, anger, and being a "victim" of life's experiences. Thus, the Fire Dragon is a powerful ally that is intense to work with and should not be engaged without acknowledgement of being ready to face your demons.

This menacing winged being will take you into the darkest parts of yourself in order to move past them and into the Light. When you are willing to move through that space, He/She will become one of your greatest allies for manifesting things into the physical plane. It is through this willingness to move into darkness, fuel it with the torch of Divine Love and dance through our illusions that we find clarity and Light on the other side. Even though the Fire Dragons feel like a menacing, almost fearful presence at times, when we see them with clarity, we realize the depth of Love fueling the fire of their breath coming straight from their Heart to us.

The Fire Dragons of Mu both male and female reside with their hearts in position of the active supervolcanos on the planet. The male is stretched through the Western United States and Canada with his heart located under the region known as Yellowstone National Park and his tail stretching through Central America. The female extends herself through most of the Indonesia Islands, her heart being located under Sumatra and her tail extending all the way through the Himalayas. She was responsible for the upheaval and tsunami that hit this region in December 2004, which brought about a great deal of chaos and one of the greatest communions of humanity with and for each other in history. This is the Light that comes from walking through the darkness. This is their gift.

To work with the Fire Dragon, take a seated posture and visualize sitting in front of or in the middle of a blazing fire. The actual presence of a fire and/or a blanket would be useful as well. Start in a comfortable position and focus on just breathing and getting yourself centered. When you feel ready, begin to chant the mantra sending the breath into the flames in all directions. You will feel a blanket of ice descend over you. This is the presence of the Fire Dragon. He/She works in opposites to what we expect.

Move your hands at this point into closed fists one on top of the other directly in front of the belly between the belly button and the breastbone. Women should have the right fist on top of the left and men the left above the right. Keep focusing on breathing and exhaling the mantra and feel the internal fire in the abdomen expand.

If the male Fire Dragon is present, you will sense a ball of fire building between the second (near the abdomen) and third chakras (the solar plexus). The female will be centered in the first and second chakras between the sex organs and the womb space. It is expected that this practice will make you extremely nauseous and so should only be done for a few minutes at a time as you gradually burn through some of the blockages and connect more deeply to the circuitry in the body that the Fire Dragon ignites.

Continue chanting the mantra and bring your focus to the fireball building within. Send the breath from your heart into the fireball to expand it and make it burn hotter. This feels ironic because you will feel the breath, just like that of the Fire Dragon coming out in arctic blasts. As the fire within builds to an icy-hot zenith, you will feel the rest of your body going frigid. Continue breathing into the fire as long as you can, the "hotter" it burns, the more pathways in the body that the Fire Dragon accesses can be opened.

You may experience lots of negative or "dark" emotions or memories come in; inhale them deeply into the heart and then with a powerful expulsion of breath, blast them into the fire. As one explodes, another older, deeper one may arise; this is a good sign that you are indeed moving into these ancient pathways and clearing them. Continue blasting them into the fire until you reach a space of relative calm within. When you have reached this space with each of the male and female Fire Dragons, then you can work to merge them.

Sit quietly in this space until you feel ready to return your focus to the physical body and the room around you. You will at this point understand the suggestion of a fire or blanket for the session. You will be chilled to the bone and a long hot shower or bath will most likely be necessary to warm you.

Take your time in expanding into the Fire Dragon energies and do not try to merge the two together too early on in your work with them. It will help to maintain a very straight upright posture in the spine. When you are ready to merge them, begin as you would normally with the breath, mantra and hand posture. Ask the Fire Dragons to merge within you when they are ready. You will feel small fires begin to build in both areas of the abdomen. When both are present, begin to send the breath alternately into each fire, building them each slowly. When they are each roaring and you start to feel extremely cold, you will know the two are close to merging.

When the two merge, you will experience a large fireball in the entire lower half of the torso that shifts the body from ice to fire with a powerful explosion and fills you with a sense of power or surety within yourself. This becomes the place from which you will manifest your creations into the world. This piece becomes more clear when you reach the level of work within the Eye of the Fire Dragon.

Bask in the warmth and light of this space and feel the body warm from the inside out. Stay here as long as you like and as you bring awareness back to the physical, see if you can still feel this new internal glow return with you.

THE WATER DRAGON

- » Associated with Lady Nada
- » Function: transmission and connection through dimensions; the conductor
- » Stone: Aquamarine
- » Metal: Silver
- » Mantra: Mee Ray An Nu Ah Tu I

The Water Dragon is our connection to All That Is. He/She is like the umbilical cord to our flow of Light, codings, transmissions… the conductor for the flow of information and unconditional Love. As such, He/She becomes a crucial link in the descension of our full Lightbody into the physical plane.

This is what our "ascension" process is really about. The descension of Heaven to Earth and that happens as each of us "descend"

our fully Lightbody into this dimension. Gaia, too, is going through her own "ascension" by descending her Lightbody and so the Water Dragons of Mu become a key link in the re-connection of her umbilical cord, which has been clamped off by the presence of Tiamat for billions of years.

The Water Dragons are the largest of the Dragons of Mu and it was the task of the female Water Dragon to reconvene the Council of Mu for the first time since the formation of the planet in order to begin the final phase of healing for Gaia and humanity. The female Water Dragon lies deep in the ocean floor with her head just off the coast of Peru holding in position a large portion of the southern Pacific Ocean, while the massive male lies under the entire Indian Ocean. They are resplendent serpentine creatures with immense power and even greater softness. They are a blend of the deepest lapis blue and verdant green; the color you might see if you viewed the Earth from millions of miles away.

To work with the Water Dragons imagine sitting chest-deep in the gentle waves on a shoreline, being swayed gently forward and back with the pulsing of the tide. Rock with the rhythm and let the breath follow suit. The breath with the mantra flows like waves pushing through dense masses, breaking them up, dissolving them and clearing them.

The breath travels past all these blockages opening a channel between your High Heart (halfway between the Heart and Throat Chakras) and the crystalline core of the planet. Imagine a white tube of light leading away from your High Heart and into the ocean connecting on the far end to that crystalline core and then, from there through a hole in the core that leads out to the cosmos.

Continue chanting the mantra in and out with the breath, deepening and broadening this tube of light. As this connection deepens, you will feel heat build in the High Heart and a softness flow in that is like a river of Grace filling your whole chest with a shimmering glow of Light. Soften into it and revel in the bliss. This is the work of the female Water Dragon. She helps you receive through this channel.

You will feel the waves of Love and Light arriving in rhythm

THE DRAGON WITHIN

with the pulse of her heartbeat, pumping straight from the core of the planet. As the channels in your heart and chest open to circulate this energy, you may experience tightening in the chest, heart palpitations or coughing spasms as blockages in these pathways get cleared out. Stay with it and try to synch your breath and heartbeat with that of the female Water Dragon. This may bring up tears and upwelling of deep emotions, as many of us have not experienced the receiving of Love to such a deep level.

When you work with the male, you will feel that bliss be circled through your chest and back out to the cosmos reciprocating the Love and Light back and opening the channel in the opposite direction. This is a powerful announcement to all Beings in the cosmos that you are ready to evolve! You will want to focus on expanding the tube of Light that is leaving your High Heart, which will take a deep focus and intention of the purest Love you can send out from your Being. Did you ever realize you could give so much?

With either the male or female, stay with the experience until your chest feels clear and expanded and the incoming and outgoing channels in the tube of light feel as expansive as they can be. Then slowly bring your focus back to the rest of the body and the room around you. Take time to just sit and integrate this new expansive feeling in the chest, along with any insights that came in that you might want to journal. You are now ready to merge the Water Dragons.

To merge the male and female Water Dragons, begin in the same way, working first with the female to expand the incoming channel of Light from the core of the planet and then inviting the male to expand the outward channel. Send out your intention for them to merge. When they merge, you will sense the flow of Love and Light take on a more pulsing rhythm as the tube splits from within and starts to spin around itself into a double helix of Light. You will feel as if there are infinity loops of Light running in you, through you, around you…a fantastic, wild ride on a roller coaster of Love. You will feel the untamed, thrashing ecstasy of the Dragons as they become one within you in a sea of Love. Bathe yourself in it for as long as you can.

Slowly, ever so slowly, let the sensations die down, staying acutely aware of all sensations in the body, and then just sit in quiet meditation for some time. When you are ready to return your attention to the physical body, your chest will feel vast and expansive, as if the entire universe is swimming around (or could) within it. Breathe deeply and slow, exhaling this magnificent force into everything around you.

Pay attention over the next few hours, day or days how long you can maintain this expansive feeling in the chest. It will also be interesting to take note of whether your perceptions of things around you or others perceptions of you shift at all.

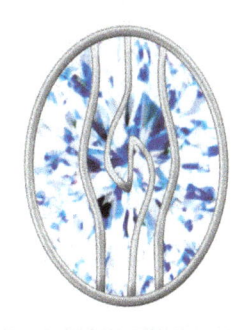

The Intergalactic
DRAGONS OF LIGHT

To begin work with the Intergalactic Dragons, sit and feel within yourself whether to work with the Black or the White Dragons first. Be sure you have already worked thoroughly with each of the Elemental Dragons to the level of merging the male and female aspects. You will find that even though the Black and White Dragons each have a male and female aspect in the physical planet, that when you work with them, they will already be merged. They hold a living example of Oneness consciousness for us: unification with individuation. Like twin flames, they are never truly separate even when physically separated.

Work with these two individually and eventually, when you feel ready, the two together. You will know when to add in the work with the Crystalline Dragon. It will be a meaningless exercise to work with the Crystalline before the other two are totally merged within you.

If you are in the physical vicinity, it is powerful to connect with the Black or White Dragons in any of the key points along the Michael Ley Line (also known as the Apollo Line) stretching from Ireland through the UK and down through France to Israel: Skellig Michael, St. Michael's Mount, Mont St. Michel, Bourges, Sacra di San Michele, Perugia, Corfu, Delphi, Athens, Delos, Rhodes, Mt.

Carmel to name a few. Their energies are intertwined through a large portion of this alignment allowing a deeper, more powerful connection to be experienced in these locations.

The ley lines running through Avebury and Glastonbury in the UK are quite potent as well for connecting with them. The same phenomenon occurs in the Pacific in working with these two dragons. There are many powerful areas, especially throughout the Hawaiian Island chain, to connect with them: Mauna Kea in Hawaii, the Iao Valley in Maui, and Mt. Waialeale in Kauai. The Tahitian islands also hold a few key power points for these two.

The trine of energies created between the Black, White and Crystalline Dragons is our connection zone between the earth plane and the interdimensional planes. It is the first level of reconnection between the points of the physical body that have been activated by the Elemental Dragons and their counterparts within the Lightbody.

It also creates a transmission space for us to access the higher DNA strand codings and have them activated, which leads to the actual anchoring of the Lightbody into the physical. Metatron is deeply associated with this aspect of the Crystal Dragon and you may sense or experience his presence in working with it.

This trine can also be called in for protection, whether you call in the Black, White and Crystal Dragons or Michael, Melchizedek and Metatron to triangulate around you. They will create a space of protection for you if you feel you are being threatened or surrounded by denser energies that are uncomfortable for you. Be keen, however, in discerning the denser energies that are external to your own versus those denser energies within yourself that are rising to be cleared or dissolved.

Once you have worked to a deep level with these energies, you will no longer need to call the trine in consciously, as you will be carrying it with you at all times. This will move you into a more peaceful, present state of being and awareness. You will see and understand situations revolving around you more clearly and without judgment or emotion. This is a pivotal step towards returning to our natural state of Oneness consciousness.

THE BLACK DRAGON

» Associated with Archangel Michael
» Works with: shadow sides, slaying, primordial power, purifying shadow debris
» Stone: Carborundum
» Metal: Gold
» Mantra: Bee Shto MI Tu

The Black Dragons lie curled up in balance with each other on opposite sides of the globe, as do the other Dragons of Mu, however they are also in perfect balance side by side with the energetic counterparts of the White Dragons. The male Black Dragon is thus in the Pacific with the female White Dragon. His heart lies near the Tahitian Islands and can be connected to there. The female Black Dragon lies in opposition balance to the White Male with her head in South Africa, her womb in Egypt and her tail curling around the Mediterranean.

The Black Dragon, like the White and Crystalline can morph its features and so may appear differently to different people. Typically they are like the other dragons with a single head, magnificent wings, powerful tail and breath of fire. However, different aspects of the Black Dragon will present different features. The Black Dragon can have at any given time one to three heads and unexpectedly breathes ice, the opposite extreme equivalent of a breath of fire capable of deep purification and destruction.

The breath of the Black Dragon is deep, throaty and menacing. It burns with arctic force igniting things held deep within the body and bringing them to the surface to be cleared. It connects us to the deepest, primordial energies locked within us and takes us into the caves of our subconscious to slay our personal "demons" – those things holding us back from connection to our true power.

To work with the Black Dragon sit comfortably with the spine aligned and begin to breath quietly. When you feel centered, it will be helpful to awaken the pathways in the body relating to each of

THE DRAGON WITHIN

the Elemental Dragons first. Do this by chanting the mantra for each in order: Earth - Mee Tu Am Na Hey Rua, Air - Mee Ru Ah Tu Nay Ah Oh, Fire - Bah Tu Haa Beesh Tau Hay, Water - Mee Ray An Nu Ah Tu I. Focus on each one individually for as many rounds of the mantra as it takes until you feel the familiar paths open that they each activate. Do this for all four. You should feel the front and back of the torso, the spine, the abdomen and the heart all tingling and open before continuing.

Now begin to force the breath into a throaty, guttural exhale and inhale imagining yourself as a huge dragon sitting in a dark, damp cave of an ancient world. When you feel fully connected to this image, begin to chant the mantra on the exhale breathing it low across the floor of the cave as if you are trying to flood the cave with the icy mist flowing through you, a mist so icy it burns. Keep this chant going for several minutes.

Eventually you will feel a thin spiral of black light coming up out of the floor of the cave, spiraling up clockwise into the base of the spine. Continue the mantra verbally until you feel the spiral reach the crown and extend upwards, stretching in both directions. Now the mantra can become internal. Continue with it as you feel the spiral grow in diameter, slowly expanding outward until it encompasses the entire body. At this point, just sit and meditate in this space. You may feel a sort of dizziness in the belly or slight nausea. This will ease and integrate the more you work with the Black Dragon.

In this meditative space, things will come to light from your deep, dark places. They are being brought up to be cleared. This is a deeper level of work that began with the emotions and memories that the Fire Dragon cleared for you. The Fire Dragon was only able to clear things blocking the energy channels. The Black Dragon can clear of all the karmic knots of lifetimes held within your DNA and cellular memory; some can even arise that are part of the collective consciousness.

Allow yourself to see them and acknowledge them without judgment or emotion. They just are. They are parts of yourself that were necessary for your journey or journeys, but can be let go of now. Hold them in front of you and breath the icy fire into them with clear intention to dissolve them completely. This is the gift of the Black Dragon.

Each time you work with the Black Dragon, more things will surface to be cleared, each a deeper layer that has been hidden possibly for lifetimes. If you feel nothing arising, send the husky breath out across the floor of the cave asking for it to move into deeper spaces and flush things out. Do this until it truly feels like there is nothing hiding in the deepest recesses of the cave.

When you reach this point, if you have already completed your work with the White Dragon as well, you will be ready to merge the Black and White Dragons. Allow yourself to just sit quietly and feel the rotating black spiral encompassing you. It holds a portion of your genetic coding and the coding of humanity. Feel its power. Feel the strength of the Archangel Michael coursing through it.

When you feel complete, allow your breathing to soften and bring your attention to the body and eventually the room. This has been a powerful layer of work. Take your time in getting up and moving about. You will most likely experience an acute sense of awareness as you move through your day.

THE WHITE DRAGON

- » Associated with Archangel Melchizedek
- » Works with: creation, grounding, solar power, activation, lineage connection
- » Stone: Opal
- » Metal: Titanium
- » Mantra: Mee Ray An Nu I

The White Dragons of Mu lay like the other pairs on opposite sides of the globe from each other, but are connected through the heart and womb channels they hold open on the physical plane. The female stretches through the mid- and North Pacific with her womb under the Ring of Fire in the Hawaiian Islands. The opening to her womb connects to us in the physical realm through the Kilauea Volcanic Crater on the Big Island of Hawaii. The male is in position curled across northern Europe with his heart channel connecting to us through the southwestern region of St. Petersburg, Russia.

Like the Black Dragon, the White Dragon can morph its features. Especially for those in twin flame relationships, the form may take on that of a 2-headed dragon: a mirror of perfect merge and balance while maintaining individuation – a true representation of our merge back to Oneness, yet bringing our individual piece. These two heads turn to gaze upon each other with the deepest Love, creating a visual image of a heart almost like a graceful pair of swans, with their breath creating an infinity loop of fire from opposite sides.

To work with the White Dragon, sit comfortably with the spine in alignment and breathe quietly for a minute bringing your focus inward. As in the work described in the Black Dragon, it will be helpful to awaken the pathways in the body relating to each of the Elemental Dragons first. Follow the guidance given in that section to do so.

Then begin to chant the mantra slowly, on the out-breath, inhaling and exhaling in a circular pattern. Exhale down and away from you forming the lower half of a circle and then inhaling from the far side of the circle up and back down to a point directly in front of the mouth. Continue the mantra for several minutes until you feel a thread of energy slowly begin to descend through the crown and into the spine.

This will be a thin spiral column of white light descending in a clockwise spin all the way down the spinal column. Stay with the breath and the mantra as long as you can. If it becomes too difficult to maintain the circular breath, just continue the mantra totally still and focus on the spiral of light entering the body.

At some point you will feel the right time to stop chanting the mantra verbally and just feel the spiral. Keep chanting the mantra inwardly and feel the spiral expand until it encompasses your entire physical form. At this point, just sit and be in that space quietly for as long as you can.

This is a deep connection to your DNA structure, your ancient lineage and all the knowledge held there for you. It is also a deep connection with Melchizedek and the power of the Sun. You should feel deeply grounded and activated in every cell of the body. This can make one feel extremely light-headed until you adjust to it. Working regularly with this energy will integrate it more quickly.

As you sit in this space, you may simply feel an elation with life and a beautiful connection with all Beings. You may also experience dreams or thoughts arise within you of things your soul longs to create, some possibly from childhood that you have long since forgotten. You may even experience some of the collective dreams of humanity.

You may have forgotten that all these dreams are possible; that you indeed can be the creative force behind them. Feel the rays of hope seep through your pores from the spiral of Light spinning around you. Feel the Remembrance come in that All Is Possible and you are on the verge of Remembering and accessing the tools to bring it about. Feel all the pathways of the Elemental Dragons tingling with life as they access the light codings spiraling around you.

Stay in this space as long as you can and when you are ready, slowly bring your focus back to the body and your physical surroundings. You will feel extremely grounded, yet giddy or "buzzing" with life throughout the day. This is the "normal" state that we have forgotten how to be in.

It will be useful to work with the White Dragon several times until this state does, in fact, feel quite normal before merging the Black and White Dragons.

MERGING THE BLACK AND WHITE DRAGONS

It is important to work with the Black and White Dragons individually until a comfort level within the body is reached with their energies. Many things will surface with both energies. When you feel ready physically, mentally, emotionally and spiritually then you can work with them together.

THE DRAGON WITHIN

The importance of this merge is monumental. This merge creates the conduit for the Crystal Dragon energies to be accessed, which is our connection between the Elementals (human body) and the Interdimensionals (Lightbody). When the trine completes, we have the capacity to anchor the Lightbody fully into the physical plane through our work with the Interdimensional Dragons. Each of us that reach this state also help Gaia to anchor her Lightbody fully for the evolution of the entire planet into higher dimensional levels.

To merge the Black and White Dragons begin first by grounding and connecting with each of the Elemental Dragons (these should have all been worked with individually already prior to work with the Black or White Dragons). Sitting comfortably, start by chanting each of the

Elemental mantras once through in succession:
» Earth: Mee Tu Am Na Hay Rua
» Air: Mee Ru Ah Tu Nay Ah Oh
» Fire: Bah Tu Haa Beesh Tow Hay
» Water: Mee Ray An Nu Ah Tu I

Then repeat each twice; then 3 times each; then 4 times each. This will take you into a very grounded place feeling the activation of the areas of the body that each ignites: the front and back of the torso, the spine, the lower chakras in the belly and abdomen, and the heart and High Heart.

Next chant in the spiral of white light down the spine of the White Dragon:
» Mee Ray An Nu I

When you feel this running down the spine add in the Black Dragon until you feel the black light spiral enter and twine around the white light spiral:
» Bee Shto MI Tu

Now begin to chant the Black and White Dragon Mantras together:
» Mee Ray An Nu I   Bee Shto MI Tu

Feel the spirals expand out together until they encompass the entire physical body. Work with this several times to reach it easily before accessing the Crystal Dragon with it, which is the next step. At this point you would chant the Crystal Dragon mantra and bring the crystal column down through the tube created by the black and white spirals, thus opening yourself to full connection and activation of the DNA and the Lightbody. Read the Crystal Dragon section before adding it in here.

THE CRYSTAL DRAGON

- » Associated with Archangel Metatron
- » Works with: sacred geometry, interdimensional ley lines, DNA, bringing formless into form
- » Stone: Diamond
- » Metal: Adamantine
- » Mantra: Mee How Tay NI Mee Ra Tu Ha

The Crystal Dragon is the core of the planet with a heart of fire and He/She is both our connection and Gaia's to the sacred geometry of Metatron, full access to our DNA and manifestation of anything into physical form. The ley lines through which we access all other aspects of the interdimensional realms pass through Her.

It is important to work with the Crystal Dragon ONLY after work with the Elementals, the Black and the White Dragons has been completed and mastered. The Elemental Dragons open the physical pathways in the body in order to receive the higher energies, and then the merging of the Black and White Dragons prepares the central channel of the spine to be able to receive the incoming crystalline structures. Adding the breath and mantra of the Crystal Dragon to the merged spirals of the Black and White Dragons brings in a liquid crystal column for transmission through the entire body.

This column runs from the Crystal Dragon in the core of the

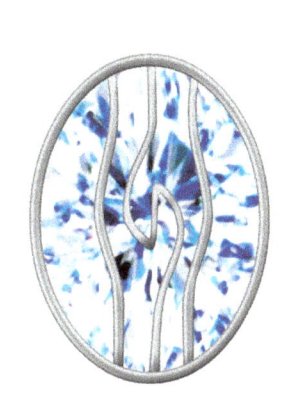

planet through the body and out to the gateway of An, the central star in the Belt of Orion. It is through this gateway that the energies from the Greater Central Sun system arrive to us. Even those connected with star systems such as the Pleiades, Sirius A or B, etc. began their journeys to the Earth realms through this gateway initially and thus connect through it to bring the higher dimensional energies to this plane in order to anchor Oneness or Unity consciousness into this dimension. This is the task we are all here for.

For those familiar with the pyramidal merkabah (8-sided: two 4-sided pyramids base to base) that is our vessel for interdimensional travel, an easy visualization is to see the Black and White Dragons holding either end at the apexes. The four points of the pyramid bases are held in place by the four Elemental Dragons. When the crystal column runs through this from apex to apex, these become the anchor points to hold the Lightbody in place in the physical plane.

To call in the Crystal Dragon, work through the breathing and mantra sequence described previously in the Merging of the Black and White Dragons section. When you feel the spirals expand out together until they encompass the entire physical body, sit in this space and just feel it for a few rounds of breath. Then begin to chant the mantra of the Crystal Dragon. You can also use the CD track of the Crystal Dragon mantra on a continuous loop, so that as you let go of the breath to just be in the space created, it will continue in the background, continuing the flow of energy in the crystal column.

You will sense a large column of liquid crystal descending through the center of the column created by the black and white spirals. This will activate the crystalline matrix structure within your cells and will feel like nothing you have ever experienced. To even attempt to describe it with human words would be a futile attempt. It will be different for every being, as each of our realities is subtly different. How can one describe the descension and connection of the Lightbody into the physical plane? Or the reconnection of etheric DNA with the physical strands in our bodies?

Sit in this space and feel the sensations coursing through you as each of the points within the channels opened by each of the

Elemental Dragons within the physical body connect to the exact same point within the Lightbody. It may feel something like a million light bulbs being turned on sequentially. Try to stay totally present with it as long as you can.

You may reach a point of utter exhaustion because this reconnection is so hard to leave and such a powerful energy to work in. It is a joyous, arduous process! It is important, though, to bring the focus back to the physical body and the space you are in. The attention has been on the physical body in a way, but not in a way that will, as yet, allow you to walk around, function, etc. in it. This will come with continued work with the Crystal Dragon. Each session will connect the Lightbody more fully; actual anchoring will come in working with the Interdimensional Dragons.

Each time you work with the Crystal Dragon, it will be a powerful experience and will typically involve some transmission downloads from your source energy, guardians, teachers, etc. This will especially be true the more work with it and deepen the connections to the Lightbody, so that more may be received.

Be prepared to have time to lay down or nap to integrate these energies. Be sure to drink lots of water and keep a circle of protective energy around you if you enter public places in the next few hours. You will be wide open as after any healing work and do not want to pick up any energies that are not yours.

Give yourself ample time between sessions with the Crystal Dragon to integrate everything that has been reconnected or downloaded. It will be best to reach a very comfortable level with this phase before working with the Gold, Silver and Copper Interdimensional Dragons.

Deeper Levels of Work
WITH THE DRAGONS

WORKING WITH MULTIPLE DRAGONS AT ONCE

There are some deeper levels of work that can be done with the dragons by working with them in pairs or multiples. It is important to complete work with each of the individual dragons first, ideally through the complete geometric grid from the Elementals to the Interdimensionals. At the very least, finish working with the dragons within one of the grid layers before combining any within that layer. For example, you can work with pairs of Elemental Dragons if you have completed work with each of the four individually before working with any of the Intergalactic Dragons.

BALANCING WATER/FIRE, EARTH/AIR

Typically when all of the elementals are present for a ritual, dance, ceremony, etc. they come in perfectly balanced in counterpart pairs. The female Water Dragon balances with the male Fire Dragon, while the female Air Dragon balances with the male Earth

Dragon. You may notice that this creates multiple layers of balance including the not so obvious aspect of winged and serpentine dragon pairs. It creates upward or downward spirals of too much velocity, likened to fanning flames or flooding lands, in either direction to have the winged dragons or the serpentine dragons work together.

This is a useful representation to follow if you are dancing with all four of the Elemental Dragons or using them as guardians to hold sacred space. Two men and two women can represent the dragons in the physical plane and call each individual Elemental Dragon in through them by using the individual mantras. If you use this, have the pairs stand opposite each other rather than next to each other, each holding a corner of the square. To really take it to another level, imagine them as the base corners of the tetrahedron merkabah and call in, in unison, the Black and White Dragons to hold the apexes. This is a powerful geometric field to work in; do not call it in lightly and be ready to go off the map with the work you are doing.

These two pairs can be worked with individually as well by combining their individual mantras and chanting the sequence repeatedly. For example, to work with Fire and Water together the combined mantra: Bah Tu Haa Beesh Tau Hay, Mee Ray An Nu Ah Tu I would be used with the same breath pattern and hand positions described in their individual sections. The same can be done with the Earth and Air pairing. There is also a track on the CD overlaying all four of the Elemental Dragon mantras that can be used for individual or group meditation work with these four.

CRYSTAL AND FIRE DRAGONS – BEESH TAU HAY MEE RA TU HA

The Crystal Dragon has a heart of fire from which its breath emanates, so the Crystal and Fire Dragons naturally interface in a powerful way. Working with the two together is one of the ways to activate the crystalline aspect of the Womb/Hara Dragon and clear any stuck energies in the lower three chakras. As we evolve, these three will actually merge into one chakra for the lower half of the body and this work does create the beginnings of evolution towards that end.

To work with these two together, sit comfortably with the spine straight and begin by just breathing and connecting to the dragon within you. Feel the breath become deep, heavy, primordial… and when you are ready begin to chant: Beesh Tau Hay Mee Ra Tu Ha (the R of Ra is rolled as on the CD Track for the Crystalline Dragon that you have already heard). You will begin to feel the pelvic floor get warm and heavy as if it is sinking into the core of the earth. Continue chanting. Next you will experience a vortex beginning to spin from the root chakra inward towards the abdominal organs encompassing the womb/hara space, the intestines, stomach, kidneys, etc. This is the fiery breath of the Crystal Dragon coming in. Visualize this vortex growing and expanding to encompass the entire lower chakra system within the body until it reaches the diaphragm level.

This vortex may make you nauseous or uncomfortable; stay with it as long as you can, continuing to chant the mantra. The Crystal Dragon is sending this breath straight from His/Her Heart of Fire as a gift to you, destroying and dissolving with the greatest Love. This energy is clearing many layers of old, stuck debris in the organs and will facilitate rapid shift if you can stick with it. At some point you may feel spirals of energy starting to expand out from the base of the vortex; this is the Crystalline Dragon circuitry in the body opening and the beginning of the womb/hara spirals coming to life.

When you feel complete for the session, stop chanting and just sit in this space for as long as you can, or stretch out and lay down to integrate the experience. Do not try to get up too soon or do this work when you have things to rush off and do in the "world". This is a very powerful exercise that deserves proper respect and time to focus on it. It will bring up whatever things were stuck in the lower part of the body, which can be daunting to discover or relive. Just let them release without emotion or judgment, honoring the part they played in your journey or previous journeys. There is no need to try and understand them with the mind.

Do not get frustrated if you can only work with the Crystal and Fire Dragons for a few minutes at a time. Continue working with them until you reach the full experience described, but be gentle on yourself.

SILVER AND WATER DRAGONS – A SONG OF HEALING HEART PRESENCE

While in Glastonbury, England, I had a wonderful remembrance while sitting at the pool of King Arthur's Court in the Chalice Well grounds. Sitting peacefully enjoying the stillness of a beautiful, crisp fall day, a chant came through that put me back into my priestess robes of Avalon. I found myself sitting by the pool and communing with Mary Magdalene and the Silver Dragon singing Ee RiaNNa Hum Na Ay over and over. The song took on a life of its own with a consistent melody for the most part, but with a freedom of octave changes and harmonics all its own. I felt a beautiful heart presence and healing come through that was that soft River of Grace both the Silver Dragon and Mary Magdalene/Lady Nada (associated with the Water Dragon) carry.

Later that same day, I wandered to visit the ancient oaks Gog and Magog that sit on the Dragon Path just East of the Tor towards Avebury. As I communed with them, I felt Magog invite me, like the young child she once knew me as, to climb into her boughs once again and be held there. Once again, as I sat in her embrace, I felt this song arise and couldn't stop myself from singing it to her… with her. I realized then its gift.

This is a wonderful mantra to sing from your heart to all of the nature beings. It brings healing not only to you, but to all of nature. You will feel it connect you deeply to the nature beings you sing it to and you will feel their hearts join with yours in celebration of it. They long to reconnect with us and heal this planet. Some of these beings have been sleeping for a long time and this can awaken them. It will also awaken the deep places in your heart that have long been asleep and afraid of such Love.

DANCE AND SEXUALITY – AN IMPORTANT PART OF DRAGON WORK

One of the only pieces I have not included in each section of work with particular dragons is their movements. This is because this is such an organic and individualized piece. Body movement and dance with each of the dragons can be a deep connective mechanism to really move the energy more deeply into the cells of the body. For those wishing to extend their work into movement, I recommend doing a round of work with each dragon in a seated meditation posture to clearly connect with the energy and the part of the body it is flowing into first. This is also because some stages of the work can create nausea or dizziness the first few times through.

Once you feel comfortable with a particular dragon and you want to add movement, start from a standing position or kneeling on all fours and chant the breath and mantra as before. This time let your body follow its own guidance into movement with the energy as it flows through. This may be different each time you work with it or a specific dance that works for you may be created. For groups, encourage the same organic, individual flow versus teaching any specific movements and have the entire group dancing one particular dragon so that not too much chaos is created with the energies mixing.

You will also spontaneously experience something akin to rising kundalini and a flow of sexual energy in working with the dragons. This is especially powerful when you are merging your energy with another dragon's energy in sexual union. It quite often will bring up spontaneous tantric flows of energy through the body resulting in full body orgasm or individual chakra orgasms depending on which dragons are present, especially if you are a DragonHeart or DragonKeeper, pairing with your counterpart. (i.e. an Air DragonKeeper and Air DragonHeart in union)

Whatever the experience, know that it is divine and moving you to release more from the body on a cellular level, allowing greater opening of the pathways in the body and cellular structures in order to anchor the crystalline grids of the Lightbody.

©Jaemin Kim

The Interdimensional
DRAGONS OF ORION

THE GALACTIC WOMB

The Gold, Silver and Copper Dragons are the Interdimensional Dragons of Orion. They are our link to the ancient interdimensional lineages, most especially the Councils of the Elohim who are directly associated with the Earth and her evolution. They carry information to us from beyond these realms from all of the star systems in the Greater Central Sun system and are assisting us in remembering our greater connection to All That Is. They carry these energies and information to us along the Solar Ley Lines emanating from the Greater Central Sun.

There are embodiers (DragonKeepers) of these dragons on the planet who are also of the Elohim lineages and associated with the specific stars in the Orion system. These dragons do walk, though, with many individuals that are very clear in their intent and integrity, even though they are not DragonKeepers. This is because these Dragons come into places going through big shifts in order to hold a presence and if enough DragonKeepers are not conscious, they will stand with any beings able to carry the energy.

This means that in the places we may consider the most dense, the most base, or the most unconscious on the planet (such as government organizations, corporate structures, places where religions dominate and control) there are energies entering those spaces on a regular basis walking with a conscious being who is working there or passing through creating subtle change unobtrusively, yet powerfully.

The Interdimensional Dragons are fully merged androgynous beings (male and female in total balance) and so in working with them you may experience both male and female presence, yet always just one Dragon in reality. They are vast beings as one would expect and powerful, yet soft and emanating the frequency of Love. Just being in their presence, one feels the truest meanings of pure Integrity, Balance, Clarity, and Love. For the sake of ease, I refer to them each as specifically He or She, depending on how the information was presented to me and which aspect of the Dragon seemed to be more present in sharing it. Keep in mind that they are truly both.

It is also important to be aware that even though you can probably access basic levels of connection with them at any point, it will be most beneficial to work first with the Elemental Dragons and then add the work with the Black, White and Crystal Dragons to that foundation. THEN adding the work with the Interdimensionals will be the most powerful and deepest connection that will lead to the most clearing, transformation, activation and anchoring of the Lightbody.

They can be worked with in any order, although working with the Gold, the Silver, and then the Copper is the most natural progression for the energies they bring. As you work with them, you will discover that they will not take you beyond levels that you are prepared to receive. This especially applies to the work of the Copper Dragon, who will be your escort into the Halls of Knowledge. There are levels of access that your level of initiation will determine naturally. As with all of the Dragons, holding an image of their symbol in front of you or in the mind's eye as you work and/or a piece of their stone or metal is extremely helpful to amplify and pull in the energy.

THE GOLD DRAGON

- » Associated with RA (Mintaka) – the right star in the Belt of Orion
- » Carries: Protection and Power
- » Stone/Metal: Raw Gold Ore
- » Mantra: Mee   Raa

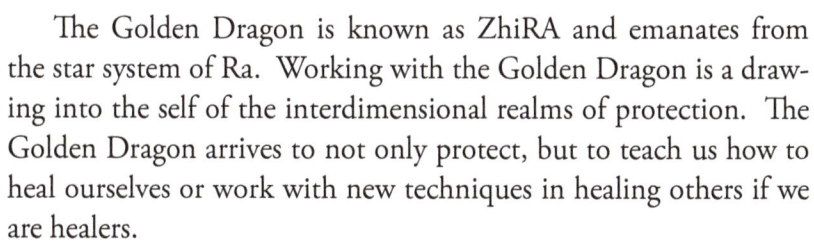

The Golden Dragon is known as ZhiRA and emanates from the star system of Ra. Working with the Golden Dragon is a drawing into the self of the interdimensional realms of protection. The Golden Dragon arrives to not only protect, but to teach us how to heal ourselves or work with new techniques in healing others if we are healers.

The Golden Dragon's female aspect is like a large, welcoming mother figure – open armed, yet encouraging of a child to grow and walk on its own. She is simply the way-shower and guide, while allowing the child's creativity and inner wisdom to be drawn out under a watchful gaze.

The Golden Dragon's male aspect becomes more of the true guardian, like a warrior at the gate, and can be called in for protection when doing work that requires deep opening to the core of your being and being totally vulnerable. ZhiRa is useful to call in especially when working with the Black or Fire Dragons when you may feel you are entering dark or shadow realms.

The Golden Dragon Breath is one of the tools He brings to connect deeply with Him and find the place of respite within. When using the Golden Dragon Breath, the body will become more relaxed and more clear with each round of breathing.

The Golden Dragon Breath is done by holding the hands up to either side of the head, about ear level, with a slight curve in the upper back so that the hands are in line with the shoulders. Press the thumb on each hand into the mound at the base of the little finger and close the four fingers over the thumb. Clench the teeth and stretch the lips apart breathing in and out deeply into the abdomen. Breathe 10 rounds of inhalations and exhalations just focusing on the breath. With the next 10 rounds add the mantra sounding the Mee (without changing the clenching of the teeth – this can be inaudible) on the inhale and the Raa audibly on the exhale. Continue with as many rounds as feels good to you aiming for at least ten minutes of continuous breath.

You will feel ZhiRa descending and standing before you; at this point you may recognize the symbol on the belly. Continuing with the breath in this awesome presence, keep breathing and sounding the mantra until you feel drawn into the Golden Dragon's belly; at this point you will be able to look down as if through ZhiRa's eyes and see the chain of diamonds symbol on your own belly.

Then relax and just meditate within this cocoon of gold. A blissful state is reached and your own golden auric field is being recharged. There should be gold bands of energy circulating up and down over your entire field until you feel ready to come back to the Earth plane. Journal your experiences, as working with the Interdimensional Dragons lends itself to different levels of experience and awareness with each session.

As you reach deeper levels of work with the Gold Dragon, you will move into the space more quickly of feeling totally enveloped in a golden sheath of light and feel the pulsing golden bands of light running up and down simultaneously over the entire field. When you reach this state fairly quickly, you can spend time there continuing to chant the mantra (your hands should stay in the fist position, but can be lowered because you will be in a deep state of relaxation) rather than just meditating.

This will continue to call in the energies of the Gold Dragon to deeper and deeper levels. This is where you will experience the beginning of the anchor points being connected to keep the Lightbody fully in the physical plane. Deeper levels of this can be reached by working with the Gold and Silver Dragons simultaneously, but work with them each individually to deep levels first.

To work with them together, begin by calling in the Gold Dragon until you feel that familiar casing of golden light surround you and the pulsing bands moving over you. Then add the Silver Dragon's mantra to this: Mee Raa…Huu Eee. Be sure to continue using the facial constrictions with the breath – jaws are clenched for Mee Raa, tongue rolled inward on the Huu, then relaxed and the throat constricted for the release of Eee.

You will feel the river of silver light enter your heart and fill the core of the golden field. Continue sounding and stay in this place as long as you can. This continues the anchoring points and connection of the etheric strands of DNA lying dormant in the Lightbody with the physical DNA strands active in the body. This exercise can be done as often as feels good to you. The more often, the easier it becomes to stay connected to the Lightbody at all times.

From here, calling in the Copper Dragon will bring you to your own book in the Halls of Knowledge (your Akashic Record) laying directly in front of you. It will be your choice to open it and slide into it for your own discoveries. Even seeing the magnificent cover that you have created for it will be a powerful tool to bring back with you by drawing it, constructing it, painting it… whatever physical form feels right for you… or none at all; simply the visual of it may be enough. For some, it may become a powerful addition to an already sacred altar space.

THE SILVER DRAGON

- » Associated with AN (Alnilam) – the central star in the Belt of Orion
- » Carries: Peace
- » Stone/Metal: Raw Liquid Silver
- » Mantra: Huu Eee

The Silver Dragon, known as RiaNNa, reaches us through the central star of An in the belt of Orion. She is the bringer of true peace in the realm of the Heart. Working with Her clears the heart and lungs of grief and ancient emotional wounding stuck there. The blood circulating through these two organs gets purified, cleared and oxygenated in a new way and the heart releases into being fully opened and centered with intent. As you breath with the Silver

Dragon, you will feel the breath move straight into the Heart on the inhale filling it with the liquid silver of the Dragon's energy field.

To work with the Silver Dragon, the hands should be laying gently in each other, palms up, in your lap, with the thumbs just touching to close the energy loop created. Typically, women will have the left hand resting in the right and men the opposite. Next, begin to focus on the breath. Curl the tongue inwards towards the centerline, rolling it upon itself as best you can, then inhale through the tube created. Now release the tongue and exhale from the back of the throat constricting the back of the tongue against the throat as best you can so the air escapes very slowly. On the next inhale, roll the tongue again, breathe in, release the tongue, constrict the throat and exhale, etc., etc. When you are comfortable with just the breath, then add the mantra.

To add the mantra, sound Huu on the in-breath through the tube created by the tongue and Eee on the out-breath with the throat constricted. It will be helpful to envision or have an actual image of the symbol on the Dragon's belly in front of you. Work with this for at least 10 minutes until you feel the actual presence of the Silver Dragon before you and see the symbol on the belly of the Dragon itself. Continue until you are absorbed into Her belly and move into a centered state of complete Heart Peace. When you reach this space you should be able to look with the mind's eye down at your own belly and see the symbol reversed there now facing outwards.

Let your heart melt and be healed. Bring to each session those things that are holding you back from experiencing true love and connection with All That Is – all other beings, be they humans, nature spirits, the Earth herself. Hold them in your heart space and feel the grief, anger, heartbreak, etc. that they cause to rise within you and breath in the Silver Dragon's healing light. Ask her to dissolve these ancient wounds for you so that you may be free of them forever. They are keeping you in duality and separation, when your soul desires to return to unity and its truest state of being.

These wounds may be from your own experience or others may rise that are healing and transmuting for the mass consciousness that has been so wounded over centuries of misuse and abuse of power: men over women, women over men… cycle after cycle of matriarch-patriarch. It is time to bring it all into balance and the Silver Dragon helps us with this. Each time we work with her we clear more debris in the collective body that has to be dissolved. We honor her by allowing this dissolution because as it dissolves more of her Silver Light can be anchored into this realm and into Gaia herself for the anchoring of her own Lightbody.

There is another experience with RiaNNa, the Silver Dragon, outlined in the section regarding working with multiple dragons at once. This involves working with the Silver and Water Dragons together. They are closely linked and you will experience one of the deepest levels of their combined healing heart presence. In a different way, this also heals the collective, but rather than the human collective, it will take you into work with the collective of the nature kingdoms.

THE COPPER DRAGON

» Associated with EL (Alnitak) – the left star in the Belt of Orion
» Carries: Strength of wisdom
» Stone/Metal: Raw Copper
» Mantra: Huu Raa

The Copper Dragon of El, known as Mazlo, comes to us with the knowledge of the ancients, most especially the ancient lineages of El who were on the planet from the beginning so that we may understand the Earth's history more clearly.

To work with the Copper Dragon, first position the fingers so that the index and middle fingers of each hand are touching each other. Allow the other fingers and thumb to collapse gently

inward toward the palms as you apply pressure to create a 90-degree bend in the two

outstretched fingers. This will almost look like two talons of a dragon's claws meeting if done correctly.

Start with just the breath before adding the mantra. Relax the

THE DRAGON WITHIN

mouth into a soft O shape and begin to inhale and exhale loudly deep into the belly, letting the breath make a lot of guttural noise at the back of the throat as it passes. Anyone listening through a doorway should be able to feel as if a dragon is sitting behind the door concentrating deeply on something. Continue this for a few minutes, letting yourself move into a deep state of relaxation.

Then begin using the mantra on an exhalation, sounding Huu from deep in the throat. This is a very guttural loud breath practice with all of the "work" being done at the back of the throat. As you inhale, sound Raa, also from the back of the throat. Continue this for at least ten minutes. It is helpful to have an image of the symbol in front of you (or in the mind's eye) as you do this.

You will at some point feel the Copper Dragon standing before you. Continue breathing until you are actually drawn into the dragon's belly at which point you can move into pure meditation. Allow the downloading of any and all information He holds for you on this particular journey together. There is great strength in wisdom and this is what the Copper Dragon brings. You are sitting in the Chambers of Knowledge and it will lead to your discovery of a different kind of strength than you have previously understood.

Each time that you work with the Copper Dragon, you will be taken to different places within the Halls of Knowledge for information that you are ready to receive. Some information may not be conscious or be able to be brought back into the physical realm in a language translatable to this dimension. Be confident that this information is downloaded into your cells and will be brought forth when appropriate.

The deepest level of work with the Copper Dragon will be accessed when you have worked with all three levels of the dragons (Elementals, Intergalactic and Interdimensional) and culminated them in sequence. This is explained in the work with the Gold Dragon and Silver Dragons together under the Gold Dragon section.

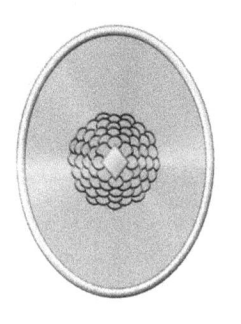

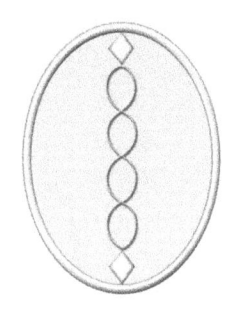

The Interdimensional
DRAGONS OF SIRIUS

THE GALACTIC MIND

The energies of the Sirian Dragons are higher octaves of the Dragons of Orion and reach us through the gateways of the three stars in the Belt of Orion: El, An and Ra. They travel in a perfect infinity loop, originating in the Sirius system, passing through the central meeting point in Orion and continuing on to Earth, then returning via the continuation of the circuit through these same points. This actually creates a perfect trine of infinity loops between the dragon lineages of Sirius-Orion-Earth. As we call upon and connect with them, these larger Solar Galactic Ley Lines become activated.

By activating these Galactic Ley Lines, a greater piece of the activation of our own crystalline matrices becomes available. With the culmination of work with the Black, White and Crystalline Dragons followed by the Gold, Silver and Copper Dragons, enough physical pathways in the body are open so that our crystalline matrix connection points can be activated in the physical body.

Diagram

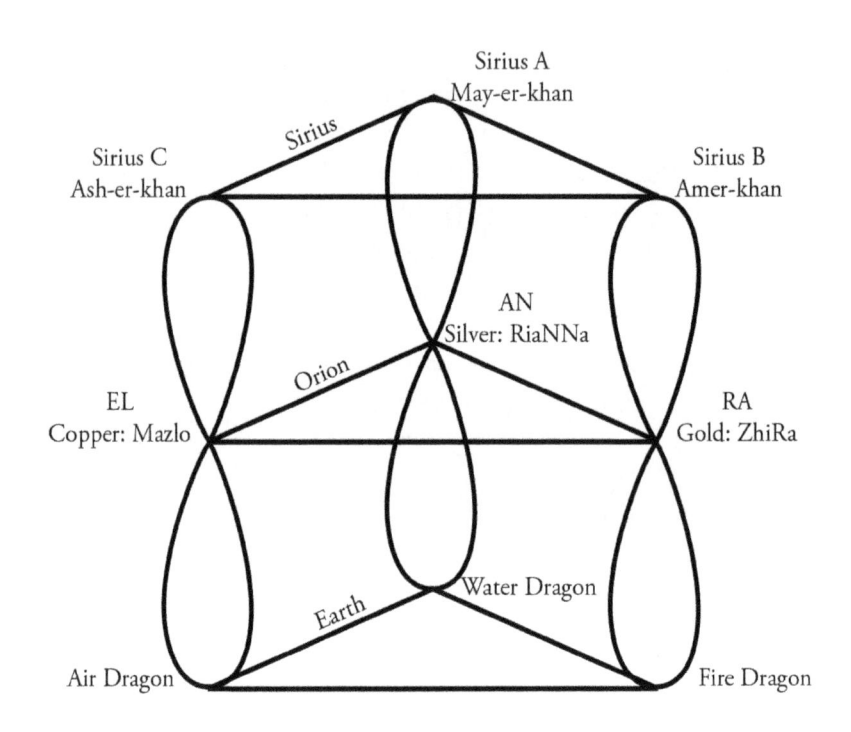

- Sirius A — May-er-khan
- Sirius C — Ash-er-khan
- Sirius B — Amer-khan
- AN — Silver: RiaNNa
- EL — Copper: Mazlo
- RA — Gold: ZhiRa
- Sirius
- Orion
- Earth
- Air Dragon
- Water Dragon
- Fire Dragon

(See expansion of this diagram on page 116)

    The Sirian Dragons then bring us the next piece; the opening of the pathways of the crystalline light geometries in the crystalline matrix of the physical body. There are 11 levels of these crystalline light geometries and all are associated with and regulated by the Elohim. Each of these 11 levels has 7 distinct geometries associated with it, resulting in a total of 77 crystalline geometries and encodings for us to access and integrate. This is the piece held in Sirius because they are the keepers of the activation of the time-piece mechanisms in the universal light geometries. Once these are opened, the geometries can be activated by direct transmission.

    As with all of the Interdimensional Dragons, they are fully androgynous beings and will be referred to as either He or She depending on the aspect that is typically more present in working with them. As you experience each of them, you may once again feel the sensation of being drawn into their bellies, as with the Dragons of Orion, yet this will differ for each person. Some may actually feel themselves at some point become infused with the liquid metal that they are made of.

THE SIRIUS A DRAGON: MAY-ER-KHAN

- » Associated with feminine side of the double infinity loop in our circuitry
- » Carries: feminine balancing
- » Stone/Metal: Liquid titanium
- » Mantra: May-er-khan Ong Ro (sung)

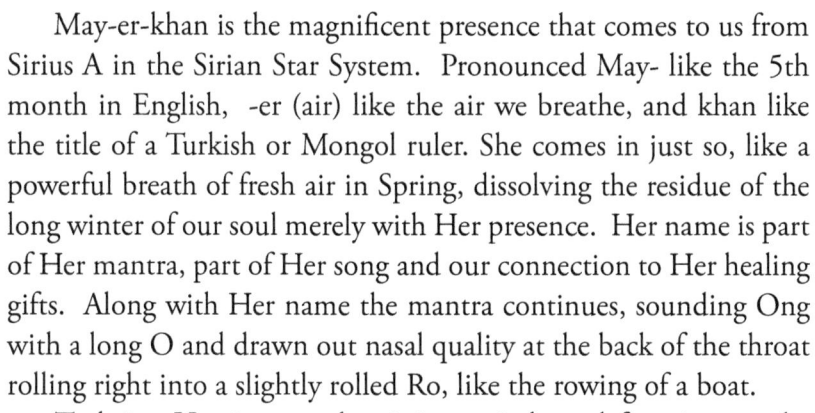

May-er-khan is the magnificent presence that comes to us from Sirius A in the Sirian Star System. Pronounced May- like the 5th month in English, -er (air) like the air we breathe, and khan like the title of a Turkish or Mongol ruler. She comes in just so, like a powerful breath of fresh air in Spring, dissolving the residue of the long winter of our soul merely with Her presence. Her name is part of Her mantra, part of Her song and our connection to Her healing gifts. Along with Her name the mantra continues, sounding Ong with a long O and drawn out nasal quality at the back of the throat rolling right into a slightly rolled Ro, like the rowing of a boat.

To bring Her in, start by sitting quietly and focusing on the breath. When you feel centered, begin to sound first Her beautiful name over and over softly. At a natural point, you will feel drawn to sound the full mantra and it will dance in and around you in its own song. As it does so, She will glide in almost inconspicuously and be directly in front of you, magnificent and immense. Stare until you can see or sense the symbol on Her belly with clarity.

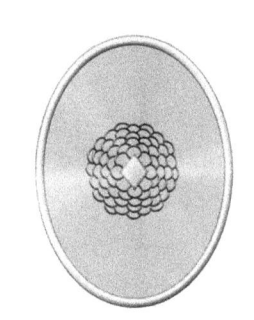

Looking into the belly of May-er-khan, one can see the matrix or expansion of the feminine form as it flowers out from the time-piece at the core of this universe. She holds the missing link, the sound and light codes, to activating the full circuitry of the womb – the Divine Feminine piece – within our physical beings (for men and women). Until this piece is cleared and activated, we cannot experience Divine Union within ourselves or with a partner. Thus She is an ultimate layer so to speak in the culmination of the work with the other Dragons in Her "lineage" – the Water, Crystal, and Silver Dragons; each being a higher octave of the other. In essence, May-er-khan is the highest octave of the Water Dragon lineage.

Keep breathing and sounding the mantra until you feel drawn into May-er-khan's belly. You may feel a slight sensation of gliding and then will realize you are within Her. Whatever your experience, once you feel you are within Her, keep sounding the mantra internally until you go into a deep space in which it lets go or sounds itself naturally. As you perceive around you, you may sense the glistening liquid titanium enveloping you and the feminine matrix almost like falling flower petals on all sides. Revel in this space and surrender yourself to be enveloped completely.

As you do, you may sense yourself going into a deep, dark space. She is taking you deeper into yourself where you may get the impression of a crystal ball or vase in front of you with a flower in it. If so, examine it – what kind of flower is it? What color? Is it open or closed? Is it rigid or soft? Wherever you find yourself, She wants to share insights with you about your true feminine nature and the state it is in. Pay attention.

Whether or not this type of information comes through, let yourself merge completely with Her; surrender to it. It may feel like simultaneous sensations of you being within Her and Her being within you. You may even feel the tangible sensation of this liquid titanium presence flowing through your cells. Whatever you experience, She is clearing, healing and activating your feminine circuitry. There may be sparks or tingling in specific areas anywhere between the third eye and alta major and the entire base of the root chakra; or just a knowing of areas in the body being worked on. Those areas where you have strong sensations are needing the most attention.

You may also sense the presence of the Silver Dragon in working with May-er-khan as they work closely together in activating the feminine circuitry in the body. Whatever the experience take note of the information She is trying to communicate to you. Stay within Her as long as you feel work continuing and when you feel it is complete, send a message of gratitude from your heart and allow yourself to slide gently back into your physical surroundings.

Each time you work with May-er-khan, more will be revealed, cleared, healed, and activated. If you feel called to work with Her, there is apparently more to be done. If you don't, be sure it is not a subtle avoidance on your part of work that a piece of you doesn't want to acknowledge.

THE SIRIUS B DRAGON: AMER-KHAN

- » Associated with male side of the double infinity loop of our circuitry
- » Carries: masculine balancing; the pattern of the Divine Male
- » Stone/Metal: Liquid mercury
- » Mantra: Amer-khan Haa Tu (breathed)

Amer-khan comes in swiftly, matter-of-factly with purpose like the other dragons of His lineage that you have already worked with – the Fire, Black and Gold Dragons. He is here to assist you in anchoring your Divine Male and activating all of the encodings in your expanding crystalline matrix that are connected to the male aspects.

Looking into His/Her belly one can see the matrix of the masculine form emanating outward from the timepiece at the core of this universe. Pronounced Amer- like the beginning of the name America and –khan like the ancient rulers in Asia, to work with this powerful being, simply sit quietly in meditation and begin to sound the name… calling Him into your sphere.

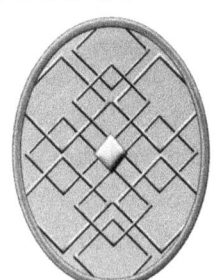

You should at some point perceive Him looking directly into your eyes and meeting you brow to brow. He is connecting through your third eye to see if you are truly ready for this activation. If you are, He will settle in front of you where you can see or sense the symbol on His belly and begin to breathe His liquid mercury form into you. At this point, begin to add the Haa Tu, sounding the Haa like a long expulsion of breath and the Tu with a long u as in the word moon. Sound the full mantra Amer-khan Haa Tu until you feel yourself gliding or being sucked into His belly.

You may perceive yourself in the midst of a field of moving geometric forms, mostly diamond-like in shape and all in constant motion. Continue to sound the mantra, asking to be taken deeper into His being. As you slide inward, you will simply feel heavy, thick, and dense. Whether or not you sense it, you are being filled with liquid mercury. Some people may only experience this level of sensation. Simply be in it as long as you can, staying in a space of total reception and gratitude.

If you experience a great deal of pain or tingling sensation at the back of the brain and in the amygdala in the center of the brain, this indicates the activation of the matrix points of the Divine Male form within you and makes sense as the male aspect is typically more identified with the mind. If you feel nothing, simply trust the process, knowing that Amer-khan is working His magic and you are receiving His gift.

If you are feeling pain, stay with it until it subsides. When the pain in the head subsides you will again feel still, heavy and dense and may alternately experience the sensation of being that field of liquid mercury and in the very next moment being suspended in the center of a cavernous void. This void is similar to the Void of Creation in the Womb of the Divine Feminine, but its feel is radically different. This emptiness feels paradoxically filled with structure and form. It is the balance needed in union with the feminine creative flow from the void of the womb to truly create.

Stay aligned with whatever sensations you are experiencing in deep meditation as long as you feel activity and when you sense a completeness, ask to be guided back out. You will once again become aware of the field of geometries in perpetual motion and with a gentle glide will be once again in front of Amer-khan facing Him. Bow in deep gratitude and ask when, if at all, it will be helpful for you to call on Him again. More than likely, it will require several sessions at specific intervals to complete the work.

THE SIRIUS C DRAGON: ASH-ER-KHAN

» Associated with activation of complete double infinity loop in the body
» Carries: Sacred Union
» Stone/Metal: Liquid Platinum
» Mantra: Ash-er-khan Ir Ma (breathed)

Ash-er-khan resides in the Sirius C System and brings to us the culmination or highest level of work than can be done with the dragons for integration into the human physical form. His gift is to merge completely the two halves of the double infinity loops of male and female circuitry within the body. If you were to transpose this set of loops from His symbol into your own core, it would extend from the crown chakra to the root.

In order to work with Him, you will begin by bringing in May-er-khan and Amer-khan first and activating their individual sparks that enliven the Feminine and Masculine halves of the loops respectively. YOU CANNOT WORK WITH ASH-ER-KHAN UNTIL YOU HAVE WORKED WITH THE OTHER TWO. In the same way that the full energies and codings that the Crystal Dragon brings through could not be received until completing work with the Black and White Dragons, without the foundation in place, the Sacred Union within that Ash-er-khan activates cannot happen.

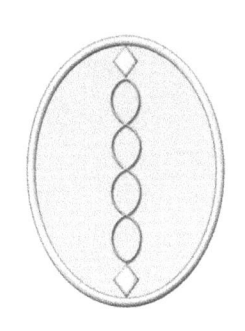

Ash-er-khan is pronounced like Amer-khan, but with an 's-h'. Sit quietly and still your breathing, getting yourself centered and open. Visualize His symbol before you in a life-size version that could fit directly into your body with the upper diamond just barely touching the top of your head and the lower diamond just barely touching the pelvic bone. This symbol is the double infinity loop of Sacred Union, the access point to higher levels in this universe, that leads the individual to the next step of accessing the DNA of the perfect human form represented by the diamond at the top of the symbol. The diamond at the bottom signifies the time-piece mechanism of our universe.

Now, begin to call in the Sirius A and B Dragons using their mantras. May-er-khan's should be sung, while Amer-khan's is breathed. As you sound May-er-khan Ong Ro, feel the first half of the double loops come to life starting at the topmost point and alternately looping down to the base, then as it rises feel the other half activate as you sound Amer-khan Haa Tu. Continue this until it is vibrating intensely.

Now add in the call to Ash-er-khan. The Ir (like ear) is drawn out with a rolled R and can be sounded in varying lengths as feels right to you with Ma being like a closure. Continue sounding all three in a round one after the other. You may begin to sense a ringing in the ears or a tingling throughout the circuit, but especially in the brain. At some point, the liquid metals of all three will create a heaviness in the body, while the spirit feels incredibly light. These are the two oppositions of duality, represented in the Divine Masculine and Divine Feminine merging, but represent all aspects of duality that are being brought into balance and oneness within your cells. This final piece within the body will allow higher levels of work with your crystalline form to begin… this leads to the expansion into the new DNA of the perfect human form.

Quite often this experience is so intense for the physical form that the body feels a need to sleep. One becomes so heavy and yet so light, that sleep seems inevitable. Let yourself fall into this so that your body can receive the highest integration. Ash-er-khan will be guiding, protecting and embracing you throughout the short sleep that will ensue. It may be only 20 minutes; it may be be longer. Let it be what it needs to be and when you come out of it sit in silence for at least 10-15 more minutes to bring it all forth into consciousness. Ash-er-khan is the only one of the Dragons that never shows us His form. He merely is felt on all levels. Send Him your gratitude, bowing respectfully to this great presence and when you are ready allow your attention to become conscious again of your surroundings. You may want to journal something, although most likely you will recall very little. The universe is paradox!

The Primordial Dragons
OF THE EARTH

TIAMAT AND THE TIAMAT TRINE

» Associated with shadow: She is the guardian of shadow

The Tiamat Trine is the trine of chaotic dragon energies located in Sumeria, Tibet and the core of the planet. The largest of the three is Tiamat. She is both the mother of form in this 3rd dimensional plane – she gave birth to the planet - and the guardian of the ascension process of Gaia since the formation and bringing in of consciousness to Gaia herself. The other two are essentially the ovaries of Tiamat. Historically, they have provided a deep connection to the most ancient dragon energies.

Unfortunately, because of misunderstanding and subsequent misuse of these ancient energies, they were closed off and lost to us for eons. The ancient Sumerians (present day region of Iran) knew how to tap into this dragon force and lost control of it. Instead of using it for the Light it could bring into the planet, their use of the energies swayed into black magic and misuse, so the channels to the dragon energy closed up.

The second time these deep, ancient energies surfaced was in the regions of Tibet. Once again misuse of the energies by the tribes people in the region was creating chaos and upheaval. The King of Tibet was frustrated at failed attempts to introduce Tibetan Buddhism to the region because of the level of black magic and dark arts being practiced. He resorted to inviting Padma Sambhava to come and tame the out of control dragon living there.

Padma Sambhava spent 13 years traveling throughout Nepal, Bhutan and Tibet clearing the demons in the region. In order to tame the chaotic dragon encompassing the area, he literally pinned it down by building monasteries along his/her spine throughout Bhutan. He thus was able to convert this dragon into being a guardian of the dharma of Earth instead of a destroyer of it. This dragon now protects beings or initiates involved in deep tantric work there, especially in the deep caves in the mountains.

Padma Sambhava was one of the first to work appropriately with the dragon energies with initiates using a practice he called dragon tantra. This was used to activate dragon circuits in the body, the Lightbody and the planet, in similar fashion to what is resurfacing now on a much bigger scale.

The depth of darkness and chaos that Tiamat was anchoring for the planet was easily felt by the greatest spiritual teachers in history like Padma Sambhava. Yeshua, for example, during the 3 days of the crucifixion consciously descended into the deepest layers of density and darkness to bring Light to those places. This would have been a journey deep into Tiamat's heart and womb. As the mother of form in the physical realm, she carries the dualities within her that define the 3rd dimensional physical plane – the pathways to the deepest darkness and chaos and the pillars of the greatest Light and unity.

As such, what we have come to realize, is that Tiamat is the primary element to Gaia's ascension and thus to our own. It will be with her release that Gaia's womb can be fully activated and her Womb Dragon awakened, which will allow her Lightbody to be anchored fully into the physical.

At present, Tiamat is wrapped around the core of Gaia seemingly smothering and hiding her secrets to the connection to life and has been so for billions of years. The keys Gaia holds were not to be revealed until humanity reached a certain level of awakening and was truly ready to move forward to the next level. It has been her task as guardian to be fearsome and menacing, like all protective mothers, lest her child be harmed by those with less than pure intention.

In initial contact with Tiamat one will experience a terrifying, almost demonic presence with a menacing red eye glaring through you, testing you. She is raw 2nd chakra energy – the creative heart of the womb. Her release will unleash a huge wave of creativity for humanity that we have blocked by being disconnected from our own wombs/haras for so long. That time is at hand and unlike previous work with her by individual spiritual masters, it is now about groups of people working together to accomplish the steps in our evolutionary journey.

Her release will be through Love. Conscious intention and surrounding her with the pure Light of Spirit is what will free her, her child and us.

TIANNU

- » Associated with light: She is the den mother, the shepherd of the dragons
- » Carries: tenderness and grace
- » Mantra: TiaNNu Ru An Nai

TiaNNu and Tiamat are twins: Tiamat is complete with the dissolution of the old, while TiaNNu reveals herself with the entrance into the new. For 5 of the great Earth cycles of nearly 13,000 years each, Tiamat has been committed to being alternately bound and released, bound and released, and bound again. With the completion of this final cycle, she can be released and the old myth of separation dissolved. The new cycle is about embracing and including her versus the old myth that she had to be rejected, slain or cleared from existence. This same myth applies to each of us and our myth of separation.

TiaNNu is the exact opposite of Tiamat in our direct experience

THE DRAGON WITHIN

with Her. They are both great, tender mothers and yet, Tiamat is the fierce protector guarding the precious Gaia, while TiaNNu is the one who holds each of us in the dragon's nest. The epitome of tenderness, gentleness, giving, nurturing… TiaNNu heals our pains and refreshes us in slumber when we allow ourselves to fall into Her nurturing embrace.

You can experience Her simply by laying in bed, both as you go to sleep and upon waking, and singing Her mantra. Ti (like the tea you drink)… aN (ahn, like the star in Orion's Belt)… Nu (with a long u)…Ru (another long u)… An (ahn again)… Nai (like the first part of night). Let the sounds find their own rhythm and melody singing from your heart to Her as a Divine Mother.

Picture Her there cuddling you against Her warm breast, rocking and comforting you like a child. Let Her mother you with soft rubbing of your back or smoothing of your hair. Begin to sense the entire nest of dragons surrounding you; they are of all sizes and colors. You may sense baby dragons jumping up and down on your legs almost like a massage of joy. Let your heart open and receive the Love they are all sending into you and the Joy they want to share with you. Revel in the nest as you fall asleep or as you wake and send a heart full of love back to them.

They will replenish you when you are weary of the toils of life, the emotional pains of the human journey, and the lonely moments when things don't seem to be flowing the right direction. Take comfort in TiaNNu as an aspect of the Divine Mother; this is Her Divine Role.

BARAHA

» Associated with balance: He is the "father" dragon in the den. Supporting, giving to the feminine, knowing he receives so much more in return; the divine example for men in the world.

» Carries: strength and courage

» Mantra: BaRaha Hu Anu

TiaNNu and BaRaha together heal our most primordial level of abandonment, rejection, exclusion and separation. TiaNNu holds the living example of the Divine Feminine before all of us, showing us by example the levels to which we can experience and emanate tenderness, grace, compassion, softness and a field of strength that underlies them all.

BaRaha holds up for us the perfect example of the GIVING male; sacred sexuality for men is about giving because they receive so much from the woman. Only the feminine can open the pathway back to the Cosmic Womb for the man when they enter the final gates in surrendered, clear, sacred union. Thus, TiaNNu and BaRaha are tangible examples for us of sacred marriage.

While in the nest with TiaNNu, if you want to pull in BaRaha and his masculine qualities to balance you and round out the healing you are receiving, or simply to feel male strength around you, when there may not be physical males present in your life, he is ready to step forward. He is always in the background when TiaNNu is present, just waiting to be called forth. Focus your attention on Him and begin to sound His mantra... Ba ... Ra... ha (all are the same short a as in Ra, the sun with differing first consonants)... Hu (with a long u)... Anu (as in TiaNNu's name).

Sound it until you feel His presence and energy flow forward in, through and around you.

THE RUBY, SAPPHIRE AND EMERALD DRAGONS OF MIDDLE EARTH

The Dragons of Middle Earth are a part of the large "family" of Interdimensional Dragons. Like the others, they are androgynous, fully merged Beings that carry specific frequencies and gifts to us in the Earth planes. They emanate specifically from another dimension of the Earth that can be thought of as Middle Earth. It is not important to understand their source in order to receive their gifts.

These three carry the most power that humans have had access to throughout any civilizations because they are the most closely related frequency-wise to our matrices in the Earth planes. Because these powers have been misused by humanity on every occasion that they have been made available, access to them is now closely guarded by very high Beings with humanity's best interests at heart, including the Christ Council and the Mighty Elohim.

The Sapphire Dragon holds space for groups (co-creation) that are committed in divine purpose (like Arthur and the Round Table – the last time work was done with the Sapphire Dragon). By enfolding each member of the group in His magic cloak, the Sapphire Dragon works with each person's specific needs for release and surrender. This allows each person within the group to bring their individual key forward to the group creation.

Interestingly, as the guardian of group alchemy, the Sapphire Dragon is also the guardian for humanity as a group with its divine intention to experience separation and strive to return to Oneness with God. The Sapphire Dragon can expedite the opening of the final gate within the human physical form to enter the gates of the Cosmic Womb that lead to reunion with God and Oneness.

The Ruby Dragon carves open the pathway between the Great Central Sun and the density of this universe, opening it for expansion of more light. Thus, on an individual level the Ruby Dragon illuminates truth and let's one see into the hearts of men (mankind). This knowledge wields great power and is one of the reason access to Her is guarded.

The Ruby Dragon when focused on the self rather than externally expands us at its deepest level into the fathomless heart. One can experience a heart-stopping explosion that allows the activation of the Diamond DNA codes in the upper chakras – an expansion of diamond grids out in every direction from the High Heart.

The Ruby and Sapphire Dragons cannot be worked with individually, but the Emerald Dragon, although limited in what She can bring without a Dragon Master present and the approval of the High Councils, can bring wonderful healing and gifts to those who want to call Her in.

THE EMERALD DRAGON: JEZ-EERA-BEL

- » Mantra: Jez-eera-Bel U Na Ru
- » Grants Individual Alchemy

Jez-eera-Bel works with individual levels of resistance, fear, and DNA activation on the journey of expansion. The most powerful magical principles are kept with Her. These are neither "dark" nor "black" magic, but as with all things could be used in this way. The Emerald Dragon emanates, as all the Dragons do, pure love and compassion for what the soul wants to experience and in revealing Her secrets, allows the individual to choose how to use Her gifts. In working with Her, she brings what each person needs in order to realize their individual dharma (purpose or Truth).

Other Dragons
IN OUR UNIVERSE

There are numerous other Dragons within our universe that can be accessed or have things to share with us or teach us. A few are mentioned below that have made their presence known, but do not have specific work to offer for the journey of opening the physical body that we have been embarking upon. There are Dragons in almost every star system and planet, so you may discover many others that are not mentioned. Those that are mentioned are simply for your reference and to share what information they did put forth. It will be your own journey of discovery to see what treasures they hold for you specifically.

THE SUN DRAGON: SORANUM

- » My name is my Mantra.
- » I am pure Light. I activate the pathway to the Sun. I work with Melchizedek and the White Dragon

THE MOON DRAGONS

- » Rahu – the South Node; the male aspect of the moon
- » Ketu – the North Node; the female aspect of the moon

Rahu and Ketu bring us great gifts, one of the most simple being the daily reminder of their sacred dance of divine union ever present before us. In simply reflecting with the moon as she parades across the night sky, if we tune into Rahu and Ketu and ask them from our hearts to come into us and merge with our beings, we will feel the dance begin within our cells that they are ever in the midst of.

It is a playful, joyful celebration of the divinely created perfect union that we all have within us waiting to be acknowledged and healed. In this dance, they are in a constant state of loving bliss. This is our inherent nature that has been forgotten and the union that we have sought for so long outside of ourselves in relationships. Until it is healed within ourselves, we cannot experience it truly with another Being.

And so, Rahu and Ketu simply dance eternally, hoping that one day, we will wake up and realize that all along they have been reflecting for us our true nature; that there has been a deeper reason behind our fascination with and cool surrender to Mother Moon's powerful presence.

THE DRAGON OF SOLARIS: NINURA

Solaris, sometimes referred to as the 10th planet, or the forgotten planet is still energetically present within our universe and is guarded by NinuRa, a majestic Dragon of serpentine form with skin that is at once Cobalt Blue, Violet-Purple, and Shimmering Diamond. She is the guardian of information held there that could be helpful to humanity to not repeat the destructive mistakes that the inhabitants of Solaris made.

THE DRAGON OF ANDROMEDA: ENNGG MAAAAA

- » Symbol: double helix of white and gold in field of cerulean blue
- » Umbilical Cord of Universe; portal to next universe

The symbol of Enngg Maaaa came through quickly and precisely when Her presence was first felt. In meditating with it, one can be taken to the edges of this universe and shown the portal to the next. When ready, this information could be useful for a soul wishing to move forward out of this plane to experience other realities or to venture there in order to bring information back to the Earth plane. Few souls are ready for this work presently, and so the symbol was not to be included visually at this time. There will, however, be souls doing this in Service to all of humanity during the next phase of its evolution and some of you may feel drawn to visualize what you may with the description of the symbol to see what it brings to light for you.

THE PHOENIX: BEN U ASR – THE CORE OF RA, THE GREAT CENTRAL SUN

The Phoenix is the culmination of all of the dragon energies together that have presented themselves to be worked with by humanity. They all originally emanated from Him and so it is in their merging and completion at the end of this cycle, that He is born from the ashes once again and will herald the new cycle of the Earth. His birth will signal a great new beginning and the calling into form of the next octave of dragons that humanity will be ready to work with as they, too, take on a new, higher vibrational form.

These magnificent beings are just beginning to manifest and are as yet shimmerings on the horizons, waiting for the Divine Timing that is called for as humanity takes each step forward. They will come forward to replace all of the dragons of this realm that have served so lovingly for so many millennia, thus releasing them for their own expansion into another octave. It will be an exciting time.

Entering the Eye
OF THE DRAGON

*I*n completing the work with the dragons through the levels with the Interdimensionals, a new layer of work can begin. This reaches into extremely powerful tools for manifestation and guidance for our Journey in the Earth planes. This work should not be entered into lightly or without clear intent from the heart space and never on anyone else's behalf.

This is your soul's opportunity to remember ancient Truths about the workings of the life force, and our co-creative powers with the Divine. This Journey is truly what You make it and you will be responsible and experience all that you choose to create. This has been true for your Journey up to this point, as it has been for the collective whole, but most of our creations have been in the super-conscious or subconscious fields.

This has allowed us to disconnect from the Truth that we have created every twist and turn, positive and negative aspect of our Journey and assign responsibility away from ourselves and blame others or external forces for the situations in our lives. Entering the Eye of the Dragon brings it to the conscious level in a very real way and you will become very conscious of what you are creating.

> **THIS JOURNEY IS TRULY WHAT YOU MAKE IT**

Each of the Elemental Dragons – Earth, Air, Fire and Water – can be worked with at this level for different things. Each brings a truly unique gift and level of deep work for your Journey. The Elementals bring us this level of work because they are the cornerstones so to speak of the sacred geometry of the planet. They are the pathways through which the manifestation of Spirit into Matter must pass and so become our link to become true co-creators with the Divine in the physical plane.

It is important to have already completed your work with all of the dragons individually through the work with the Gold, Silver and Copper Interdimensional Dragons, because the Lightbody needs to be fairly well anchored in order to move into these levels of work. There are gifts to receive that cannot come in without the advanced stages of preparation of the Lightbody in the physical. The Dragons will not receive you into the Eye if you are not prepared.

At this level, you will be working with their merged aspects and so will feel their presence as both He and She. You will be working more directly with their symbols, so having a strong visual image of them either directly in front of you or in the mind's eye will be important. You may come to the realization in working with the symbols for each that within their make-up, the Eye of the Dragon has been subtly ever-present. Each symbol will take on a new form now as you look at it from a new perspective and hold it in front of you as a portal.

Spend time first breathing with yourself. Then begin to breathe and chant the mantra of the dragon you desire to connect with. Hold the image of that dragon's symbol in the mind's eye trying to bring forth the color of the stone behind it as vividly as possible. If your heart is true and the alignment and intention in integrity, the dragon will invite you – almost pull you – in through the center of the symbol: the gateway into the inner eye of the dragon.

You may feel as though you are being pulled into a crystal ball of moldavite green, yellow topaz, carnelian orange or aquamarine. Indeed you are. Watch your breath once you have entered to be sure you are indeed still breathing. Breathing becomes more difficult in this space and initially must be forced. The multi-dimensional realm you have entered is one the physical body is unaccustomed to and will take some adjustment. This is one of the reasons having the Lightbody anchored to the physical body is crucial to move forward in your work with the dragons. Try to feel the rhythm of the dragon's breath and align with it.

Once inside this space, follow your inner guidance to a comfortable space and visualize standing or sitting, whatever feels appropriate, and when you feel the dragon focus on you, open your Heart and reveal what you have brought in with you. You will need to be truly Open and ready to receive. This is a vulnerable space to be in, but should be quite comfortable after the work already achieved and received from the dragons to open all the channels within the body and anchor the Lightbody.

Working with the Elemental Dragons of Mu in this way has been their dharma waiting to unfold and come forth and so they revel in it, but not without caution. You will not enter the Eye of any of the Dragons if you are not ready or if your Heart is not true. This has been the turning point for many civilizations; the testing ground if you will. Each reached this level and as each revealed its true desires and intentions of misuse or lack of Heart connection, the Dragons of Mu shut off the channels of connection and assisted in the destruction of the civilization. It will be up to us the direction we take this time.

THE EYE OF THE EARTH DRAGON

Entering the Eye of the Earth Dragon brings us into a magnificent space of manifestation. One enters here to create. What do you wish to manifest into your life? What dreams do you hold as yet unrealized? What lies deepest and dearest in your Heart that you want to bring forth into the physical? This is the place to bring them.

Begin with the breath, finding your center and pulling yourself into the moment. Keep a visual image of the Earth Dragon symbol in the mind's eye. As you reach your center, add the Earth Dragon mantra: Mee Tu Am Na Hey Rua, sending the breath out across the floor and roof of the cave as in earlier work with the Earth Dragons. Feel their energy descend down the front and back of the torso, pulsing through these channels in a now familiar way. Send out your intention to the Earth Dragon that you would like to enter the Eye of the Dragon for a deeper level of work with Him/Her.

Continue chanting the mantra until you feel the Earth Dragon approach and incline its head down to the floor of the cave in order for you to enter the portal of the symbol that leads into the Eye. You will sense a glowing, green field surround you, as you enter and move further into the Eye. The moldavite glows a brilliant earthen green from an undistinguishable light source within the Dragon. (If you are unfamiliar with moldavite, visit a gem shop or search the internet to have a vivid picture of this color in your mind.)

Sit or stand in what feels to be the center of the Eye. Continue to breathe; it will feel more difficult here to do so. Try to synchronize your breath with the Dragon's breath. When you have been deemed ready, you will feel the attention of the Dragon address you and ask what it is you desire to manifest into the physical plane. Be ready to reveal it in full detail. It is wise not to enter here with mere empty-handed curiosity. The Dragon does not take lightly to being disturbed without aim.

Creation can only happen from the heart and womb space connection. Feel your dream, or dreams, growing from the deepest desires within your heart, and let them bubble forth in the presence of the Earth Dragon. Once they are out in front of you, He/She will guide you to gather them all in your embrace and pull them down to the base of the womb space. Hold them here and feel their depth. It is wise not to bring in too many to each session. Focused attention to one creation is usually the most truly productive.

You may feel the base of the womb space begin to grow warm or experience a lotus flower expanding upward and blossoming here to hold this dream in its central vortex. This will be the space this dream gestates in until its birth into the physical plane. Hold it here and breathe with it. Feel the Dragon's breath and yours inhaling and exhaling as one, encircling the space with a warm, gestative mist. Then, just breathe in harmony with the Dragon. Feel the pulse come to life within the dream being held here.

Hold it as if embracing a child or as a pregnant mother would hold her belly, lovingly, tenderly, expectantly with such a deep feeling of connection to this child from the heart space at the same time.

At some point, you will know it is time to leave your creation in the safe hands of the Earth Dragon. It will gestate here until each aspect of it is ready to come to fruition in the physical plane. This place is still within you and you carry it with you at all times. You may even at times, experience physical symptoms as if something is growing within the womb space.

You will feel the Earth Dragon lower His/Her head so that you may exit and find yourself once again in the cave where He/She lives. In deep reverence, bow in gratitude to this great Being who has assisted you in a powerful manifestation. Be in this space as long as you feel necessary to integrate, comprehend, process, remember it all… then exit the cave and bring yourself back into the physical realm.

Feel the creation within you that has returned with you. You may feel heavy. This is a good sign that what you want to create is truly grounded into the physical plane now. Rest assured that this creation will birth at exactly the right time.

You will want to continue work with this dream by entering the Eye of the Fire Dragon. This will release the deepest roadblocks and illusions that have been holding or will hold this dream from manifesting, which you are most likely unaware of and lie deep within you. Working in the Eye of the Fire Dragon will fuel the manifestation to its next phase.

THE EYE OF THE AIR DRAGON

Entering the Eye of the Air Dragon brings us into a ring of total clarity. At first, as you enter there is great mental confusion. You can't really tell where you are or if you are in the right place other than the orb of yellow light surrounding you. This is in divine and perfect alignment because in order to receive the gifts of the inner eye of the Air Dragon, you will be called to enter the clearest space you can define within yourself. It is in this place that we can empty the mind and feel almost a complete submission to the space of knowing nothing. When we arrive, the Air Dragon's attention can turn to us and answer all the questions within our heart.

This is a space that allows true understanding without emotion of all life situations past, present and future that we have incarnated into: subtle family structures and dynamics, relationships both positive and negative, business partnerships or relationships. The list is endless because we are endless as is the knowledge and understanding we seek of our dharma in this lifetime. Until we understand what we are doing here, we can't truly step into doing it in a fully conscious, powerful way. Understanding the past and present gives us clarity into the now of what we are manifesting in each moment, as well as the direction to follow to truly achieve our life's purpose or dharma.

This can be a daunting and scary place to be if you are not ready to truly understand with absolute clarity the dynamics of the life situations you have created. This is why the work within the Eye of the Dragon is not lightly taken on. And will not be successful if the Dragon deems you unready to receive the level of the gift He/She brings.

To begin this deeper work with the Air Dragon, begin in a comfortable position and focus on the breath. Take the mind to a calm, clear space and when you feel stillness descend begin to chant the mantra using the breath pattern and mantra used with the Air Dragon in previous work: Mee Ru Ah Tu Nay Ah Oh. Because you are working with both the male and female merged, you will find the breath wanting to be exhaled in counter-clockwise vortices both skyward and towards the floor. Simply alternate this pattern until you feel the familiar line of energy opening through the spine channel and have connected with the Air Dragon. Keep a visual image of the Air Dragon symbol in the mind's eye at all times.

Then continue chanting the mantra and visualize this magnificent creature standing before you. Ask to be allowed to move into a deeper level of work with Him/Her and enter the Eye. Continue chanting the mantra, verbally or internally, moving into a deeper and deeper space until the Dragon lowers His/Her head in order for you to step through the portal within the symbol and enter the Eye.

If the Dragon does not receive you, simply accept this knowledge without judgment or self-criticism, knowing that you in fact are the one deeming yourself unready to know the answers to the questions you seek. When you are truly ready, you will be allowed to enter and you will know when to try again.

If you have entered the Eye, move as deeply into the center of the space as possible. You will be encased in the gleaming light of the yellow topaz center, surrounded by amber, which lends golden-brownish threads of light to the atmosphere. You may feel confusion and uncertainty as to whether you have really arrived in the right place. Am I really in the Eye of the Air Dragon? Or am I merely in a deep space? The warm glow and golden tones of the light around you will be your guide.

This is the Dragon's way of forcing you to find true inner stillness, for it is only in that space that you can receive with absolute clarity the stream of consciousness He/she can bring through into the physical for you. As the confusion subsides, you will feel that stillness arise from a space deep within your core and it will feel like Home. Even just reaching this space is a great gift to take back with you.

At this point, you feel the gaze of the Dragon's inner eye turn upon you and bid your Heart to open its basket of questions. With each, simply let the stream of consciousness come through in whatever form it takes for you to receive information. Not everyone receives in verbal format. Some may receive sound, color, or sensory information; chunks of "knowing" are the most common. Some downloads come embedded in code as transmissions through the third eye channel directly into the mind. These can create an uncontrolled fluttering of the eyelids as they arrive. Simply be aware that this information is being downloaded and you will receive it through dreams, synchronicities or intuitive hits at the appropriate time.

When you feel complete with the questions and answers you have brought – try not to bring too many at once or trite questions about decisions, etc. in your life – this information is a deeper level of understanding of all the soul's purpose and journey in relation to all the relationships it encompasses. If you understand these aspects, the rest will fall into place in your life without effort.

As you prepare to return to the physical plane with full consciousness, graciously thank the Air Dragon for working with you and wait for the signal to exit. It will be clear and you can then slowly exit the Eye, returning to the cave first and then returning fully to the room around you.

Keep a journal of the questions and answers that you received, so that as future questions arise, you can link the information for broader understanding without burdening the Dragon with questions you have already received information about.

THE EYE OF THE FIRE DRAGON

To enter the Eye of the Fire Dragon requires a space of deep humility. In this place, you will be able to see the truth of the roadblocks and illusions that have been holding you back from your dreams and heart's desires. It is helpful to have already worked within the Eye of the Earth Dragon, so that the dreams you have placed into gestation there can be worked with. It is these that will have a kindling of the fire below them, incubating and gestating them by working within the Eye of the Fire Dragon.

Hold the symbol of the Fire Dragon before you and begin to breathe, pulling yourself into a clear, centered space within the body. Visualize yourself sitting in the cave of the Fire Dragon as you begin to chant the mantra: Bah Tu Haa Beesh Tau Hay. As you exhale, send the fiery breath out in all directions. When the Fire Dragon enters the cave with you, you should feel the abdominal and pelvic channels opened in previous work with Him/Her flood with energy. Send out your intention that you would like to enter the Eye of the Dragon in your work with Him/Her.

You will feel the Fire Dragon looking straight through you, sizing you up in a way. You will not be allowed to enter until you sit in a space of complete humility in His/Her presence. This is because once you enter, you will need to be in complete humility in your own presence as you face the black mirror.

If you have been deemed ready to enter, the Dragon will lower its head to you and you will see the magnificent carnelian eye before you, with just a thin black slit down the center. Wait for this to expand into a full doorway and then enter. You will be in a black hallway with no light. Keep moving forward until you feel an orange-red glow form around you. You will be standing in the center on a large disc – the black mirror.

You will feel the Dragon's attention turn inward to focus on you and begin to address your dreams or more realistically what is holding you from them. You will be asked to start examining one by one the roadblocks you think stand between you and your heart's desire. Work with one dream at a time. As you unveil them, you will begin to realize that what you thought were the roadblocks really have no bearing; these have been the false illusions keeping you from looking deeper. Realization will dawn, because you will hold each one in front of the black mirror and you will see its Truth. The Dragon will assist with this sorting and guide you to cast it aside, hold it aside to look at later or examine it more closely.

Keep digging and revealing until you find the root block that is the real cause. It will most likely be linked to an ancient fear you hold deep within about yourself and/or your behavior in the presence of the arrival of this dream in your life. This can be a shocking and unexpected revelation. Allow yourself to look at it honestly and without judgment, in gratitude that you can finally with awareness of it, be free of it. Lay it on the mirror.

When the core illusion has been revealed, the Dragon will show you the inner chamber within the eye. You will see or feel a wall of fire with another black doorway in the center rise before you. Enter this deeper space. This is the cool center where you will be held safely while the illusions left out on the black mirror are burned away.

When the process is complete, you will feel the black walls around you drop and you will once again be standing in the carnelian glow on the disc of the black mirror. Are there any more dreams and illusions to look at today? If so, hold the next dream out to the Dragon and begin to look at the roadblocks holding you from it.

If you are complete with the knowledge that has arrived, the Dragon will begin to breathe with you to fan the flames around the dream you hold in your womb that is gestating. This is why it is prudent to have worked within the Eye of the Earth Dragon previously, so that you do have a dream already being gestated into the physical plane through the womb and not just held in your heart as a hope or longing. This will expedite its journey and this is how the Fire Dragon becomes a power source in fueling manifestation.

When you feel ready to return to the cave, bow in deep gratitude to the Fire Dragon and as His/Her head lowers to the cave floor once again, step out and slowly find your way back to the physical space around you. You will most likely feel very warm and a deep emptiness in the body. This is because you have just undergone a deep purification.

> YOU HAVE JUST UNDERGONE A DEEP PURIFICATION

This purification and burning up of illusions begins and ends in a clear state of deep humility. It is from this place that we can truly express honestly with ourselves, and others, and so this work reminds us what that place feels like and deepens our daily communications because we learn again to speak from this space.

Besides the wonderful gift of clearing the path for our dreams to come to fruition, the more we work within the Eye of the Fire Dragon, the more we return to our ancient bases of communication within, to and for each other.

THE EYE OF THE WATER DRAGON

To enter the Eye of the Water Dragon will require you to move into a state of pure, open, Heart presence. In this opening, you will be able to receive and experience the magnificence of boundless unconditional love. This is the gift that in receiving you feel bound to share in service to humanity and Gaia. By becoming a vessel in the space, you become a transmitter of this frequency that the planet so desperately needs at this time. Like a Lighthouse, this will beam forth from your Being and affect all you pass by.

Begin by finding a comfortable seat and moving into the breath. When you feel centered, add the mantra of the Water Dragon: Mee Ray An Nu Ah Tu I and visualize the symbol of silver and aquamarine. As you sound the mantra, send out your intention to the Water Dragon that you would like to enter the Eye in your work today.

Then begin to move deeply into your Heart space, opening and softening, opening and softening. If the Dragon does not lower His/Her head for you to enter, you are being asked to move deeper into the Heart and open even more. There are recesses in the Heart some have never reached and this is the depth you need to go to. Even experiencing this depth of your own Heart space can be enough for one session. It is an experience to master, especially before the experiences that will come within the Eye.

When the Dragon's head does lower, you will see the beautiful aquamarine iris surrounding a pupil of silver. Enter this space and begin to move down the hall. It will feel like you are surrounded by silver and almost feel as if there is something moving in the shadows just out of your peripheral view. If you look closer at the hallway, you will see that to all sides of you are mirrors reflecting all aspects of yourself throughout your lifetime.

Some of these are easy to look at, especially in the deep Heart space you are in, while others will make you question yourself. You are being asked with each that you pass to embrace and love that aspect of yourself wholeheartedly. This may be difficult. You will see yourself at all ages in all kinds of interactions: a teenager being

THE DRAGON WITHIN

rude to a bus driver or store clerk, a spouse yelling at a child, a child throwing dirt at another child… the list is endless and only in your experience. There will be many that you had forgotten about.

Look carefully at each one and love them anyway knowing the divinity and perfection you were created in as a divine reflection of God in the physical. After you have embraced what you thought to be all of them, as if to magnify this point, the final mirror will be a reflection of you totally naked. Can you embrace this as well and realize that it, too, is a divine reflection of God in the physical? You will only move into the center of the Eye and out of the hall of mirrors when you can truly embrace and love them all.

If you succeed, you will begin to see a glowing blue field surround you of translucent aquamarine like the brilliant bright turquoise of a Caribbean bay. Stand or sit in the center and feel your heartbeat synchronize with the Dragon's; the breath and pulse aligned as one. Then you will begin to swim in the river of Grace that is unconditional love. This frequency is like a Homecoming and one of the most blissful spaces we can move into. You may even sense or hear the sound of an angelic choir coming from the heights of the blue sphere you are in.

As you receive and fill yourself you will begin to realize that as it enters and fills you, so is it exiting through you, through every pore in your body and out in all directions. Begin to visualize all the people, situations, leaders, places in the world, etc. that you want this to go out to. As you think of them, they will appear in the walls around you as if to validate for you that they are feeling it.

Stay in this place as long as feels good to you. The more you come here, the more of this frequency will be anchored in all the cells of your body in order for you to be like a transmitter of it as you move through your daily routine. You are never actually disconnected from this stream, but having a conscious place to go in and replenish or connect to it is a helpful way to remember this greater piece of ourselves.

This is the gift that the Water Dragon has been holding for the planet and for humanity, waiting for the right time for it to be opened. Water – the best conductor available and the largest portion of our body and the planet are made of it…little coincidence in that. It is the conductor through which the transmissions of the frequency of unconditional love can move instantaneously through the physical planes.

Revel in this space and return to it often. Each time you will be tested in the same way, not so much as a test, but more as a preparation to clear the body completely to receive at the deepest level. This is what all of the "tests" the Dragons bring us through are about. They do not want to deny us any of their gifts. They have waited for eons to share them, but know the harm they will cause without the proper preparation or initiations.

When you are ready to leave the session, turn your attention to the Water Dragon and send out a wave of gratitude, acknowledging what you have received and asking to be allowed to enter again in the future. You will feel the passageway begin to open into a silver hallway that will take you back out. As you exit, you can slowly begin to bring your conscious focus back to the physical body and the room around you.

You will feel heavy at first from the depth of the space you have been in, but as you return to full awareness in the body, you will feel light, almost giddy as if there is an elixir bubbling through your veins. That childlike wonder of our youth returns with it and a playfulness of spirit that will last through the day (or longer). You may experience others looking at you inquisitively as if trying to figure out why you look so different today. Smile inwardly knowing that your Lighthouse is shining and they just can't put a finger on what it is. You are bringing a great Service to the world!

SUMMARY CHART OF THE DRAGONS

Realm	Dragon	Association	Purpose	Stone	Mantra
Earth	Earth	Ishtar	grounds manifestation into physical	Moldovite	Mee Tu Am Na Hey Rua
	Air	Kwan Yin	transfers info/energy into consciousness	Amber & Yellow Topaz	Mee Ru Ah Tu Nay Ah Oh
	Fire	Isis	burns up blocks, fuels manifestation	Carnelian	Bah Tu Haa Beesh Tau Hay
	Water	Lady Nada	conductor for info/energy flow	Aquamarine	Mee Ray An Nu Ah Tu I
Intergalactic	Black	Archangel Michael	purifies shadow, primordial power	Carborundum	Bee Shto MI Tu
	White	Archangel Melchizedek	creation, activation, grounding	Opal	Mee Ray An Nu I
	Crystal	Archangel Metatron	activating crystalline matrices/geometries	Diamond	Mee How Tay NI Mee Ra Tu Ha
Interdimensional					
Orion	Copper	EL-left star in Orion's belt	wisdom, Halls of Knowledge	Raw copper	Huu Raa
	Silver	AN-center of Orion's belt	peace, heart opening to unconditional Love	Raw liquid silver	Huu Eee
	Gold	RA-right star in Orion's belt	protection and power, amplification	Raw gold ore	Mee Raa
Sirius	Sirius A	Feminine aspect	feminine balancing	Liquid titanium	May-er-khan Ong Ro
	Sirius B	Masculine aspect	masculine balancing	Liquid mercury	Amer-khan Haa Tu
	Sirius C	Sacred Union	activation of double infinity loop	Liquid platinum	Ash-er-khan Ir Ma
Earth's Core	Tiamat	Shadow	guardian of shadow		
	TiaNNu	Light	den mother of Dragon's nest, imparts tenderness, grace		TiaNNu Ru An Nai
	BaRaha	Balance	carries strength and courage		BaRaha Hu Anu
Middle Earth	Ruby	Merlin	illuminates truth		
	Saphhire	Arthur	group alchemy		
	Emerald	Morgaine	grants individual alchemy		Jez-eera-Bel U Na Ru
Sun	SoRaNum				SoRaNum
Moon	Rahu	South Node	exemplifies loving bliss of inner union		
	Ketu	North Node	exemplifies loving bliss of inner union		
Solaris, 10th Planet	NinuRa		guardian of information for humanity		
Andromeda	Enngg Maaaa		umbilical cord of universe, portal to next		

115

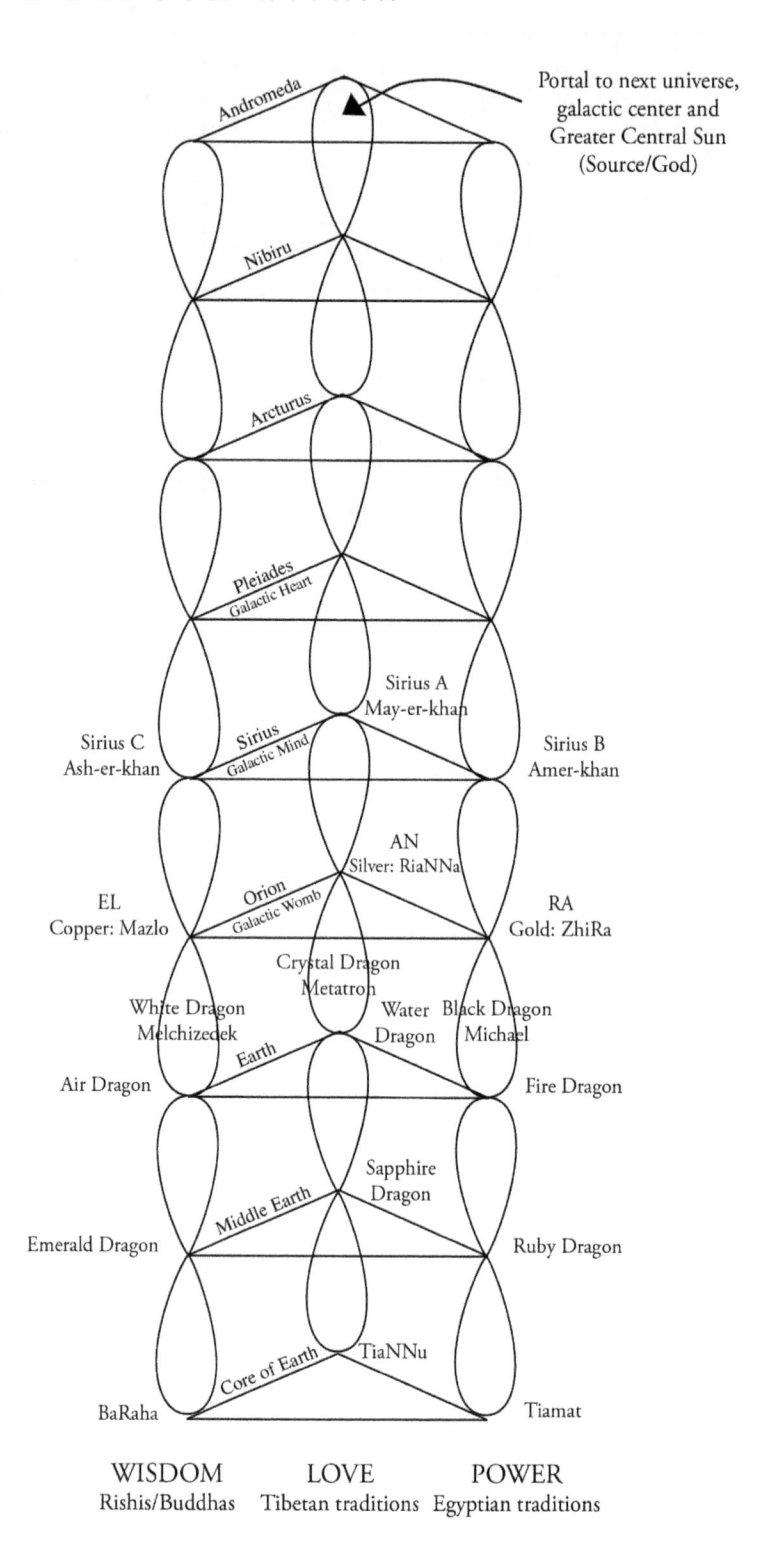

THE DRAGON WITHIN

Portal to next universe, galactic center and Greater Central Sun (Source/God)

Andromeda

Nibiru

Arcturus

Pleiades
Galactic Heart

Sirius A
May-er-khan

Sirius C   Sirius   Sirius B
Ash-er-khan   Galactic Mind   Amer-khan

                   AN
                Silver: RiaNNa

EL   Orion   RA
Copper: Mazlo   Galactic Womb   Gold: ZhiRa

                Crystal Dragon
                  Metatron
        White Dragon   Water   Black Dragon
        Melchizedek   Dragon   Michael
                        Earth
Air Dragon   Fire Dragon

                  Sapphire
                  Dragon
                Middle Earth
Emerald Dragon   Ruby Dragon

                        TiaNNu
                Core of Earth
BaRaha   Tiamat

WISDOM   LOVE   POWER
Rishis/Buddhas Tibetan traditions Egyptian traditions

116

DRAGON HIERARCHY/ENERGY FLOW WITHIN OUR GALAXY

This diagram indicates the lineages of the dragons as well as the flow of energies coming to us from the Greater Central Sun. Each star system is a stepping down station (or stepping up for the reverse flow) for the energies to be translated into a usable form by the next level in the hierarchy of the lineage. Our evolution and descension into the 3D realms of the Earth planes came successively through each of these systems and as our ascension process progresses, the higher vibrations and information of each of these systems becomes available to us once again.

As explained under the Geometry of the Dragon Energies section, at higher vibrational levels, the light/energy waves are very short and fast, while those of the the lower levels are longer and slower. Thus, with each step-down the wave gets longer and slower.

Currently the Dragons have revealed themselves to be worked with through the level of the Sirius system. A few have made themselves apparent in the higher systems, but the majority of humanity is not ready to work with them and the higher energies they carry and thus their work has not been revealed. This will come through and be revealed in a second book most likely or in a workshop environment.

Each of the lineages is associated with one of the core foundations of Love, Wisdom and Power; the balance of which allows evolution. So, moving up the lineage for example of Love, we find the higher and higher octaves of this energy exemplified through TiaNNu, the Sapphire Dragon, the Water Dragon, the Crystal Dragon, the Silver Dragon and the Dragon of Sirius A, May-er-khan. The dragons within trines or within lineages often work together as you may discover during your journey with them.

The Black, White and Crystal Dragons as shown in the Geometry of the Dragon Energies section are a bit special as they triangulate with the Archangels at the level between Orion and Earth.

General Questions

MALE VS. FEMALE DIFFERENCES – USING THEM BOTH

You will discover in working with the Elemental Dragons that there are specific male and female aspects of each that come forth. These are described in each section for the specific Elemental Dragons, as well as how to merge them and what experience that may bring. For many aspects, it needs to be an individualized, organic process, as each dragon shares with us in subtly different and unique ways.

The difference between the experiences for men and women is mainly in the Womb/Hara Dragons being activated. This, however, as described by men in the Womb Activation circles is a fairly similar experience to the women in the group. They feel the same physical sensations in the womb space and the same type of creative power awakening; they also definitely have a name for this space like all of the women do.

Men will experience these things, but typically it will be the women called forth to awaken and activate these energies first in order to then awaken the men. I, for one, applaud all the men out there that are leading the way in this realm.

WHY ARE PEOPLE SCARED OF DRAGON ENERGIES AND THEIR USE; OF DRAGONS THEMSELVES; ARE THEY DEVIL WORSHIPERS/EVIL ENTITIES?

There has been a lot of fear generated over centuries around dragons and it would be natural for many to be fearful of using their energies. It is locked in our cellular memories from the Crusade eras when the dragons were driven from the planet (see below). All beings, including humans, in this dimension carry the duality of density (or evil as some call it) and Light in their nature. It is inherent that all beings can express either characteristic. The majority of animals will only move into aggression when put into a defensive position.

The dragons gained a reputation as fearsome beasts because they were being hunted and defending themselves. Their truest nature is as loving protectors. Even Tiamat, who is the mother of chaos and form – the most dense energy available – is at her deepest core full of the greatest Light. It is in her protective role as Mother that we disturb her and thus feel the wrath she can carry.

When you connect with a dragon for the first time coming from your Heart space, you will understand the deep Love that they carry because they come from the same Source we do.

WHY DID THEY DISAPPEAR FROM THE PLANET?

Fears arose during the Crusade era regarding the dragons, created by a regime that wanted to crush out all nature worship, whether it was for trees, the Goddess, the Earth or animals, including the dragons. There were crusades to hunt and slay them along with their worshipers. The dragons disappeared because they were no longer understood or wanted here. They still exist in the mists and many are sleeping in the hills surrounding the countryside of Europe, for example. Many energy workers, in the last decade especially, who have a dragon connection, have been finding themselves coming across dragons in the hills ready to be awakened.

INDIVIDUAL WORK VS. GROUP WORK; LOCALIZED VS. SACRED SITES

All of the dragon energy exercises described in this book can be done individually or in group settings. As with most energy work, group dynamics add exponentially to the energy experience. Working with a trained facilitator is even more powerful, as is working on-site in sacred sites or locations of high earth energy, such as those described on the Michael Ley Line through Europe. There are many powerful sites in the world where you will feel particular dragons more powerfully than others in those areas. You do not need to travel all over the world, though, to experience the power of your connection with the dragons. Wherever you are, they are waiting to meet you and will come to you.

For answers to lots more questions, there is now a full compilation of live videos on the Dragons play list on my YouTube channel.

Acknowledgments

Thank you to Padma for the awakening and remembrance he facilitated within me to the magnificent dragon that I am; without this, none of this information so long buried would have been able to surface in order to be shared with the world. I am eternally grateful as well for his assistance in grounding in the project, pushing me to see more, editing and most of all supporting my personal process with it all.

Thank you to my parents who consistently unconditionally support the twists and turns of my journey and the friends who listen and support without question – Bev, Gail, Carol – making it possible for me to expand ever deeper into this journey.

Thank you to my sister for the loving care of my beloved furry friends so that I could be away for extended lengths in the creation of this work.

Thank you to Angie (TiMonRa) and Whitney (AnRa) for their incredible conscious artwork on the cover and symbols.

Thank you to Rachel for translating this work so perfectly, graciously and with so much love.

Thank you to Solara and her work that allowed the beginnings of these awakenings within me.

Most of all, I have to thank all of the Dragons for sharing their knowledge, love and secrets with me… without them, truly this information would not be here.

About the Author

Hello. My name is Araya AnRa. Like you, I am many things; on a daily basis I wear many hats as friend, mother, sister, teacher, student, employee, business owner, healer—but each one of those is only a very small aspect of the tangible thread of Mother/Father God that each of us is. We are so much more!!

I have failed many times. I have been shattered many times. Each time, in the wake of healing, I find myself rising anew like a phoenix; each time reborn to a higher aspect of myself; one step closer to knowing and realizing God's perspective of who I truly Am. With every step in full surrender and a heart-driven desire to expand, my connection to everything beyond the physical plane expands. The clarity crystallizes of the next step, the underlying block, to whom or where I need to turn for assistance. We all have pieces for each other. God's perfect Law of Attraction brings our perfect mirrors before us (as angry and ugly as they may seem). IF we are willing to look deeply into them, healing and shift can happen.

My real opening to myself began in 2002. Some inner voice was guiding me to quit my job and take time to go within. I was terrified, had a mortgage and lots of animal friends to feed, and not a clue how I was going to pay the bills. It was the most transformative time I can point to that started the journey of awakening for me. It was in the cloister of that cold, snowy Wyoming winter that I reconnected to my Self as a healer. It was as if I was remembering things I knew how to do long before being born into this body.

Exactly 9 years before that, I learned how to meditate at a Buddhist monastery in Southern Thailand and then set it on the shelf. Now meditation would become the doorway to knowing my guides and my future freedom. Talk about a powerful tool in the tool belt! The experience of learning the art of meditation was the 180-degree turn that has led to so many others since then. I began teaching and sharing meditation in February of 2003, a full 9-year cycle later, based on guidance during my own practice and a surrendering to the inner voice of Spirit trying to align me with my soul purpose.

Even with a whole new set of tools by 2012, I found myself shattered again. I felt like my life blew up after finally getting to a place where I was living my dream co-teaching workshops and giving sessions all over Europe. I lost my marriage, my work, my belief in myself... and found myself coming back to Reno, because that's where my family is, feeling like an utter failure and totally lost, and having to hold it together for my 3-year old son.

We can go the slow route. Or we can get launched forward. Both are appropriate at different phases of our journey. It took me four years of inner cocooning to recover and heal from the explosion. It is miniscule in the bigger picture of our journey to Love. And then I could again feel my guides tapping me on the shoulder and saying 'It's time. Let's get moving forward again.' So I started listening and trusting again. With two pre-arthritic thumb joints, I enrolled in a reflexology certification program. Ten sessions into the practicum, it became crystal clear why.

I found all of my energy work and psychic gifts that had been put on the shelf for a spell beginning to bridge with the physical work happening with the person on the table. I understood the new beautiful paradigm of the whole package being healed and shifted all at once. And I found my connection to the other side stronger and more clear than ever before, the energy flowing though me equally so and my desire to be in service to springboard growth in others that much greater.

From there the flow was in motion lie the Truckee River in the spring thaw. Remote session clients kept finding me through my old website, my new reflexology clients were having big shifts before my eyes and as happens when we are in the flow, synchronicities just kept aligning for the next step and the next step and the next step. Thus was born Invoke Healing International. My small vision was going to be much bigger than I had expected! And now, it justs keeps growing through my Facebook community and word of mouth.

So Who Am I? First and foremost I am a child of Mother/Father God on a journey Home. My personal expression of God is as a healer, a harbinger of change, a catalyst and bridge to removing blocks and finding greater Truth for each of the souls that feel ready to dive in.

Araya is a certified Psychic, Medium, Angel Channel and Energy Healer by the American Federation of Certified Psychic Mediums and a certified Reflexology Practitioner through the Universal College of Reflexology. She is also affectionately known by some as The Dragon Lady, as she has a unique relationship with the Dragons that allows her to guide others who experience the Dragons to understand them, connect with them and be healed by them.

It was in September of 2007, after attending a workshop in Kona, Hawaii, and activating her connection to her DragonHeart Self that she found herself led to Glastonbury, where she was able to bring through this tremendous guidebook to work with the dragons —The Dragon Within—which has facilitated new levels of opening for all of its readers.

Dragon's Breath CD TRACKS

1. Earth
2. Air
3. Fire
4. Water
5. The Elemental Dragons
6. The Black
7. The White
8. Merging of The Black and White Dragons
9. The Crystal
10. The Gold
11. The Silver
12. The Copper
13. Ee RiaNNa Hum Na Ay

To get your digital copies of the CD mp3 tracks, please go here:
https://dragonwithin.com/dragonsbreathcd